Secretarial Office Solutions
A guide to problem-solving

Secretarial Office Solutions

A GUIDE TO PROBLEM-SOLVING

**BERNADETTE CHANIN
AND LYNN HULL**

McGRAW-HILL Book Company (UK) Limited

London · New York · St Louis · San Francisco · Auckland · Bogotá
Guatemala · Hamburg · Johannesburg · Lisbon · Madrid · Mexico
Montreal · New Delhi · Panama · Paris · San Juan · São Paulo
Singapore · Sydney · Tokyo · Toronto

Published by
McGRAW-HILL Book Company (UK) Limited
MAIDENHEAD · BERKSHIRE · ENGLAND

British Library Cataloguing in Publication Data

Chanin, J.B.
   Secretarial office solutions.
   1. Office practice
   I. Title   II. Hull, J.L.
   651   HF5547.5

   ISBN 0-07-084651-0

Library of Congress Cataloging in Publication Data

Chanin, Bernadette.
   Secretarial office solutions.

   Includes index.
   1. Secretaries. 2. Office practice. 3. Problem solving.
   I. Hull, Janis Lynn. II. Title.
   HF5547.5.C46   1982   651.3'741   82-17263

   ISBN 0-07-084651-0

12345   86543

Typeset in Baskerville and Univers by David John Services Limited · Maidenhead · Berkshire and printed and bound in Great Britain at the Cambridge University Press, Cambridge.

To Brian and Alan
for their inexhaustible patience
and constant encouragement

Contents

Preface for the teacher   ix
Preface for the student   xi

Part One   **The human element**
   Unit 1   Getting to know people 3
   Unit 2   The right approach 14

Part Two   **The importance of good planning**
   Unit 3   Are you sitting comfortably? 27
   Unit 4   At all events 39
   Unit 5   Meetings are a little more than terminology 52
   Unit 6   Planning a safe journey 68

Part Three   **Where to find it?**
   Unit 7   Can you find it? 83
   Unit 8   It's knowing where to look 97

Part Four   **Keeping it safe**
   Unit 9   A potentially dangerous environment 109
   Unit 10   Taking precautions 119
   Unit 11   The true meaning of secretary 130

Part Five   **Still about people**
   Unit 12   The personnel function 139

Part Six   **What of the future?**
   Unit 13   People or machines 155
   Unit 14   Where do I go from here? 171

Index 177

Preface for the teacher

This book is intended to be used for those students who are studying for any of the following qualifications:

- RSA Diploma for Personal Assistants
      (Personnel and Functional Aspects)
      Secretarial Duties, Stage II
- LCC Private Secretary's Certificate
      (Office Organization and Secretarial Procedures)
      Private Secretary's Diploma
      (Private Secretarial Duties)
- BEC National Diploma
      (Secretarial Services Option)

and any other courses run at junior executive level involving people and office management.

Rationale

We identified the need for such a book when working as a team, teaching secretarial duties in a further education establishment. Our students varied greatly in age, experience, and academic achievement, but they had the same goal. Time was short because of the breadth of the syllabuses and the steady application needed to assimilate all of the facts, yet we felt some time must be devoted to what we considered to be a vital area of secretarial training — the development of problem-solving ability. The mere provision of model answers, while time-saving, did not help the students to discover for themselves principles that they could apply to problem-solving in general.

Success was achieved by presenting students with problems on which they were able to work with the teacher in a supportive role, when ideas were flowing freely, but who was available to give guidance using questioning techniques whenever help was needed.

A great deal of ground was covered in this way because students either worked in small groups on different problems and then pooled ideas, or parameters were set within which students were able to work on a self-help basis.

By working in small groups, students developed curiosity and respect for each other's thinking, flexibility in ideas, and the capacity to think laterally. Students also acknowledged that they found this method of getting to grips with realistic problems stimulating and thought-provoking and that eventually they were able to think beyond the obvious bounds of the problems.

The book itself

With this method the onus is on the teacher and we have tried to reduce the amount of preparation by providing credible and viable problems that, while adhering to the requirements of examination syllabuses, vary not only in length but also in complexity, thus enabling the teacher to select those suitable for different levels.

The guided answers are the hub of the book in so far as it is these guidelines that will encourage the student to think beyond the obvious and which show that there need not be any one correct answer — a fact many students find difficult to accept. There are in addition plenty of unsolved problems to give students further practice.

It is therefore hoped that teachers will find the book a very beneficial addition to the many excellent textbooks available on secretarial duties and that it will be useful for students working in small groups at their own pace, or individually in class, or even in their free time!

Our experience has shown that students *enjoy* problem-solving. We hope *you* will enjoy using this book.

Preface for the student

This book is intended for use after, or in conjunction with, a recognized factual textbook on secretarial practice. It is not intended that this book should provide you with the standard facts that can be found in such textbooks, but rather aims at encouraging you to use those facts and the knowledge you have gained in order to solve the type of problems that arise in everyday office life.

Your life at work will be no different from your social life as far as problems are concerned. Nothing runs smoothly forever, no matter how carefully planned, because no one has yet found a way of planning for the unforeseen occurrence.

While many difficulties can be avoided if you are well-organized, problems that do occur can be overcome if they are approached in a systematic manner.

Our aim is to help you to develop this way of looking at specific problems and adopting this approach when faced with problems in real life.

Layout of the book

Each major section is made up of one or more units — each one on a given topic — and each unit is set out as shown below.

Introduction   A general text to introduce you to the chapter and to give you a guide as to its content.

Do you know?   A checklist to help you to verify what you do or do not know before you proceed any further through the chapter. There is, therefore, still time to learn if you are not sure.

Snippets   This part contains useful facts and tips.

Short problems   Two or three short problems, usually of a factual nature, which are followed by our suggested solutions. You should try to answer the problems before checking with the answer.

Long problems   These may take the form of case studies, assignments, or problems and have guided answers that are designed to try to help you to develop a logical approach to problem-solving.

One step further These problems do not have a guided answer, but where possible they are extensions of those that have a suggested approach. By working on these, you should therefore be able to assess whether your ability to solve such problems has improved.

Part One

The human element

1

Getting to know people

Father, Mother and Me,
Sister and Auntie say
All the people like us are We,
And every one else is They.

KIPLING (1865-1936)

We all have a mental picture of what epitomizes a certain profession and we are influenced a great deal by characters depicted in books or magazines, or portrayed in films and on television, or by people we know personally, who do a particular job. You may have your own preconceived ideas of what a secretary should look like and the work she should do.

By dictionary definition, the word 'secretary' means a 'person employed by another to assist with correspondence, literary work, and other confidential matters'.

In reality it is a blanket term that describes many different jobs in both large and small organizations. It may be used at one end of the scale to describe someone engaged purely in typing and transcription, handling the telephone, filing, and other minor duties, in other words to describe *a shorthand/audio typist* (who may have been given the title of 'secretary' to enhance the status of the person for whom she is working).

At the other end, it may be used to describe someone who does neither shorthand nor typing but who is involved, among other things, in organizing and participating in committee meetings, arranging and then accompanying her boss on journeys, and being involved in long-term planning, in other words to describe *a junior executive or personal assistant.*

Whatever skills are used and whatever knowledge is needed for a specific secretarial job, we believe that in addition to the necessity to develop the ability to problem-solve, the good secretary must be able to interrelate well with people.

In all secretarial posts there is, to a greater or lesser degree, involvement with people and it is the extent of this involvement that may influence your choice. If, in an attractive-sounding job, it would be necessary for you to work with a lot of people, but you are a shy, diffident person, happiest in a one-to-one relationship, you may decide that this would not be the job for you. On the other hand, you must remember that even in a small company, working for one person, your circle of contact will always include others.

Can you be self-critical?

You should be aware that communication barriers may be created by a clash of personality types and that an understanding of behaviour patterns may help you to appreciate these problems and other emotional factors that may affect performance. In addition to developing a greater understanding of other people, such a study may also help you to recognize and refine any personality difficulties you may have and that affect your interpersonal behaviour.

Have you stopped to consider how *you* see yourself and how you think *other people* see you? Are you aware of the interaction between people both in communicating verbally and non-verbally?

- In your social life, as well as in your business life, are you sensitive to your effect on others as well as their effects on you?
- Do you think that the way you behave towards people affects the way they behave towards you?
- Do your family and friends whom you treat with warmth, respond warmly?
- Does the girl in your group whom you don't like and to whom you are hostile respond in the same vein? Are you perpetuating a situation by not making an effort to 'get to know' the girl?

In your social life you are probably able to dismiss or to avoid people with whom you don't get on. In business this is not always possible. Unless there are to be constant personality clashes with the resultant effects on performance, job satisfaction, and even on health, constant efforts have to be made to understand people and to enable them to understand you. In a secretarial capacity you will have a wide sphere of contact from the chairman to the office junior and you may also have a supervisory role. Whatever the situation, you will be responsible for trying to maintain harmony among those around you.

Role adjustment

If you think about your own role in relation to your teachers, your classmates, your parents, boyfriends, and friends with similar interests, you will perhaps gain an insight into how you adjust your role to the different situations in which you find yourself.

This instinctive ability to adjust to different people in different situations in your personal life will be essential in your business life where you must adjust your role to a number of people at varying levels.

To your superior you must present the image of an efficient, well-organized person, overtly dominated but — depending upon the relationship — covertly dominant.

To your juniors you must still be efficient and well-organized, but also approachable, able to delegate, and overtly dominant.

Perhaps only with your peers can you be completely relaxed and your true self and then only in the absence of other factors such as competitiveness or fear of criticism.

How does this adjustment to your role show? Involuntary actions very often give away what one is thinking or feeling. When you consider the myriad meanings that can be conveyed by facial expression, body movement, and body posture, it becomes clear that everything we say and do is representative of our inner feelings — that is, if we allow involuntary actions to take over.

In business, however, it is important to be able to control those natural reactions and adjust to what is really required in order that the work in hand can be carried out in the most efficient way and the desired conclusion reached. In effect, one must learn to work within the parameters of the job role, and in this way a good 'image' will be maintained at all levels.

Do you know?
1. What influences you when meeting new people? Are you impressed by clothes, voice, apparent status and achievements, social graces, personality traits — or none of these things?
2. What gestures *you* habitually use in non-verbal communication?
3. How you would define 'personality'?
4. The correct way to greet visitors and put them at ease?
5. What is meant by 'rapport'?

Snippets
1. Even in the fourth century BC Hippocrates suggested a classification of personality into four types:
   Melancholics   prone to sadness and depression.
   Cholerics   prone to anger and irritability.
   Sanguines   prone to cheerfulness and optimism.
   Phlegmatics   prone to being emotionally stable and controlled.
2. Carl Jung defined people as either:
   Introverts   those interested mainly in their own mental processes and enjoying their own company, and who are considered to have a longer attention span.
   Extraverts   those whose interests are in objects and matters outside of themselves.
   Most people are **Ambiverts**.
3. **Self-image**   how a person sees and thinks of himself.
   Self-esteem   how a person values himself.

Short problems

1. This morning your boss, the personnel manager, is due to interview applicants for the post of trainee in the reprographics room, and will be interviewing at half-hourly intervals starting at 10 a.m. with the last applicant due to arrive at 12.30 p.m.

At 10.15 the receptionist calls to say that a young lady has arrived for interview at 10.30 but the heel on her shoe has broken and she is in a distressed state.

How would you deal with the matter?

2. You are the assistant manager of a large business equipment showroom that occupies a corner site at the intersection of two busy roads. Through the showroom window you witness an accident between a motor cycle and a car. Both drivers escape unhurt but considerable damage is done to both vehicles. You are convinced it was the fault of the car driver. He, however, angrily blames the cyclist and storms into your showroom to see if anyone witnessed the crash. You recognize the car driver as a director of a company that is one of your major customers.

What would you do?

Suggested solution to problem 1

This is a matter that must be dealt with on a face-to-face basis.

1. Go down to reception and, using her forename, try to calm her down and reassure her that the accident will not jeopardize her chances at the interview.

2. Look at the shoe and try to assess how seriously it is damaged.

3. Call maintenance and see if a man is available to do a running repair if one is possible.

4. While waiting for the maintenance man, you and the receptionist could ring around for any alternative footwear available. Scholl sandals? Driving shoes left in the car? Reassure the young lady that even if the shoes look incongruous they will not mar her chances of success.

5. *If alternative shoes are found,* ask the receptionist to arrange for the junior to have the damaged shoes repaired, checking first on available repairers and the prices charged. Ensure that the applicant has sufficient cash or alternative means of paying. Return to your office with the young lady and explain the incident to your boss before the interview commences.

6. *If alternative shoes are not found,* return to your office at 10.25 in order to show the 10 o'clock applicant out of the department. Inform the personnel manager of the problem encountered by the next applicant and ask if the interview could be delayed until 1 p.m.

How do you think the secretary has to adjust her role throughout the situation? Would you have handled the matter any differently if the applicant had come for a more senior position?

Suggested solution to problem 2

1. As the car driver is in a state of shock, try to calm him down. Encourage him to sit down and offer a sweet drink or cigarette (if he smokes).

2. Ask one of the assistants to call the police — vehicles causing an obstruction.

3. *If there are other witnesses:*
- You could avoid admitting that you saw the accident but does anyone else in the showroom know that you saw? Would this mean your losing face and credibility?
- Does your conscience still dictate that you must admit and make a statement that may mean the possible loss of an influential client?
- When your customer is calmer could you talk with him and make him understand that as a citizen you must do your duty?
- Are you the only witness who thinks it is the fault of the car driver?
- Did you in fact see everything that happened? Did anyone outside the showroom have a closer view?

4. *If there are no other witnesses:*
- It will be the car driver's word against the cyclist's unless you intervene.
- Be non-committal to the driver — give a private statement to the police if called.
- Could you persuade the driver to admit that he is in the wrong and cool the situation by suggesting a possible settlement out of court?
- You must not antagonize the client unnecessarily but still do what your consience dictates and not lie.
- You must be able to combine the role of citizen with that of assistant manager.

Long problem

You are a qualified farm secretary working on a temporary basis for Messrs Bolton, Howard, and Clarkson, who have a very busy veterinary practice in a market town in Devon.

David Bolton and Karen Howard are on duty. They specialize in treating both large and small animals. The third partner, Michael Clarkson, is abroad on holiday. The veterinary nurse, Anne Mason, is unfortunately away with a virus infection.

At this moment the surgery is crowded and the telephone rings yet again! It is a local farmer (who regularly uses your practice) phoning to tell you that his best cow is calving and appears to be in difficulties.

How would you deal with this situation?

Suggested approach
For the purpose of this question let us assume the following:

1. That one veterinary auxiliary is on duty.
2. That a queuing system is in operation.
3. That the farmer is very level-headed — and this call indicates a high degree of urgency.
4. That there is still half an hour of surgery time.

What emotions and attitudes might this situation arouse in you?
For a new or temporary secretary, unfamiliar with the regular clientele, the initial reaction might be *panic* at the realization that you are at the centre of this many-faceted situation.

After this may follow concern, firstly with regard to the cow, and then for the other clients who are going to have a longer wait if one vet goes out on a call —and the possible reaction when you inform them of the situation!

These emotions, however, must not be allowed to show too much. You must appear to be calm, confident, and clear-thinking in this stress situation.

What is your sphere of contact in this situation?
Jot down the people in your sphere of contact and analyse how you would need to adjust your role when dealing with them. Then check your list with Fig. 1.1.

How would you deal with the situation?
Below is a step-by-step approach to dealing with this awkward situation. Don't read on until you have tried to work out *your* approach.

1. Calm the farmer and assure him of your immediate attention. Take all the relevant details and extract the records for that animal.
2. Approach the first vet to be free and give him all the details.
3. Help prepare any instruments and medication he may need.
4. Inform the remaining vet and veterinary auxiliary of the situation.
5. Start to re-organize:
  (a) Explain the situation to waiting clients.
  (b) Animals for new dressings to veterinary auxiliary.
  (c) Animals for injections and routine check-ups — either to veterinary auxiliary or arrange an appointment for another surgery.

(d) Carefully integrate remaining clients onto vet's list in order of arrival to avoid conflict.

(e) Try to estimate length of waiting time.

6. Telephone the farmer as soon as the vet is en route to enable him to estimate the time of arrival.

7. New arrivals must be informed of the situation and possible length of wait. Gently persuade them to return to the next surgery unless really urgent. Above all no client must be peremptorily turned away and every client must be offered the choice of either waiting or going.

If dealt with in this way, with the right attitude, a good impression is created and maintained both of you and of the veterinary practice itself.

Farmer	Overt dominance — authoritative, calm, reassuring, instilling confidence and a sense of efficiency that the matter will be speedily dealt with.
Vet concerned	Overt subservience — subtly showing dominance, clarity and confidence in presentation of facts, knowledge of vet's personality and needs, helpful.
Other vet	Covert dominance — persuasive, reassuring, helpful, calm, efficient.
Veterinary auxiliary	Overt dominance — authoritative but pleasant and persuasive, not belligerent (a panic symptom).
Clients (a) *Already waiting*	Overt dominance — placatory, sympathetic, command attention, group dealing, confidence and efficiency.
(b) *New arrivals*	Overt dominance — counselling and listening, authoritative.

Figure 1.1   Your sphere of contact in this situation and the role adjustment needed.

One step further

You should by now realize that had the assumptions made been different, then in some respects the approach would also have been quite different.

Work through the problem again using the following assumptions:

1. The farmer is neurotic and liable to panic.

2. A system of fixed appointments is in operation, but there is flexibility in the system for sudden ailments.

3. There is still one hour of surgery time to go.

4. Anne Mason is on duty as well as the veterinary auxiliary.

Long problem

In your position as secretary to the industrial relations officer in a company that manufactures various sorts of breakfast cereals you come into contact with the people on the shop floor and are usually asked to be present (with their consent) during meetings in order to take notes and so help your boss. This morning a shop steward came into your employer's office to warn him that morale on the shop floor was getting extremely low and that there would very soon be problems. Until now employee relations in the company have been good. The shop steward indicated that the problems lay with the new production manager. He left the following list of complaints:

- All requests for time off — even for dental visits — have to be in writing.
- Anyone more than five minutes late in a month has his name displayed on the noticeboard.
- Workers are blamed for failure to meet production targets.
- No talking is allowed except at break-times.
- He insists on all workers calling him 'Sir'.

1. What mental picture have you of this person in his role of production manager?
2. How would you endeavour to verify that the claims were true without arousing the suspicions of either the production manager or the workforce?
3. Why were the points listed above having a demoralizing effect?
4. What, if you were asked, would you suggest to rectify the situation?

Suggested approach

As the question is in four parts, take each one individually.

What mental picture have you of this person in his role of production manager?
You should be able to subdivide your assumptions about this person into:

Appearance
Character and personality
His background

and then analyse why you were able to make such assumptions.

Under each of these headings list the features you can see in your mind's eye. Our ideas are given in Fig. 1.2.

Appearance	Dark suit and crisp white coat; handlebar moustache — plastered hair — well-manicured hands; in his late forties or early fifties; not particularly tall.
Character and personality	Authoritarian — strict disciplinarian, totally inflexible with regard to rules and regulations; elitist ('them' = workers: 'us' = managers); poor communicator and motivator of staff; a theorist; self-righteous; hierarchically aware; petty-minded.
His background	Ex-service officer; good paper qualifications; 'upper middle' class.
Based on:	Information given; media portrayal of authority figures; what society demands of managerial positions; first-hand experience of such people.

Figure 1.2 The mental picture you might have of this person in his role as a production manager.

How would you endeavour to verify that the claims were true without arousing the suspicions of either the production manager or the workforce?
Needless to say this must be undertaken with a great deal of tact and diplomacy. Information to verify the claims raised by the shop steward may be gleaned not only from the production department itself but also from other departments.

Give some thought to which departments may be able to help:

- By observation and subtle discussion, possibly with the production manager's secretary.
- Sales, stores, and personnel (for bonus purposes) may also be able to help with regard to the alleged cause of a fall in production.
- Discreet questioning of other personnel authorized to enter the shop floor, e.g.: quality control, machine maintenance, research and development, and organization and method.

Why were the points listed above having a demoralizing effect?
You should be able to justify all your answers to the questions given below.

1. Assuming that members of other departments are not treated in this way, what emotions have been aroused in the production workforce?
2. How would you imagine the workforce feels towards the production manager?
3. Is the workforce likely to be affected by other employees?
4. What is the likely interaction between the employees in this department?
5. Are there any other peripheral factors likely to affect their attitudes?
6. Is the working environment likely to be affected?

7. Are the answers to the above questions likely to aggravate the situation from the production manager's point of view?

The following are the keywords that should guide you when answering the above questions:

School children	*Hostility*
Demotivation	*Boredom*
Resentment	*Ridicule*
Barriers	*Piecework*

What, if you were asked, would you suggest to rectify the situation?
Although we think it is unlikely that you would be asked to make suggestions of this nature, we feel you should follow the problem to its logical conclusion.

Cover up the remainder of this section and try to work out each step to be taken. Uncover and check as you go along.

Step 1 Assuming you have verified that the facts are indeed true, report back to the industrial relations officer (IRO) with your findings.

Step 2 The IRO contacts the personnel manager, informs him of the situation, and suggests he sees the production manager.

Step 3 The production manager must be made aware of the industrial unrest and the possibility of strike action.

Step 4 The personnel manager *must* allow the production manager to have his say as to why he has introduced such measures. (The previous production manager may have been lax.)

Step 5 A meeting should be held with the personnel manager, production manager, and shop steward to reach a compromise solution.

Step 6 In order to restore respect for the production manager, whatever compromise is agreed, it must be presented as company policy so that it is clear to the workforce that it is not another whim of the production manager.

This is a good example of someone playing a pre-set role to the full and it should be appreciated that this person may be totally different in another situation.

One step further
What measures could the production manager take to win back the respect and cooperation of the workforce?

How could he develop and ensure the maintenance of good relations in the production department?

Additional problems

1. Your employer's assistant, a departmental manager, is constantly having to replace his junior secretary. Your employer is very concerned about this and knows that each girl has talked to you of the difficulties and her reasons for leaving. Although this has been confidential information to you, you feel that the time has now come when your employer should be aware of the difficulties and, in your capacity as his secretary, you also feel that you should offer comments on how the situation could be improved. State how you would approach your employer and express the difficulties experienced by other secretaries. (LCC PSC)

2. You are secretary to Mr Charles Fortune, sales manager of Dexel Electronics, a company that manufactures highly specialized electronic equipment and that has rapidly increasing sales in the UK and a developing export market.

   At 10.30 your employer has an appointment to see Mr David Mitchell, buyer in a UK company. This is a last minute appointment at Mr Mitchell's request and he is aware that your employer's time is limited to one hour.

   At 11.30 Mr Fortune has an appointment with Mr Kushida, a buyer from a Japanese company that is a prospective customer and therefore an important contact. Your employer intends to take Mr Kushida to lunch and to follow this with a tour of the factory and demonstrations of the equipment in which the latter is interested.

   Mr Mitchell did not arrive at 10.30 and after waiting half an hour, your employer has left the office to talk to the works manager about Mr Kushida's visit.

   At 11.20, the receptionist telephones you to tell you that your two callers have arrived: Mr Mitchell having been held up in a long traffic jam caused by a serious car accident and Mr Kushida to keep his 11.30 appointment.

   How would you deal with this difficult situation?

3. You are the training officer in a large organization. A group of students accompanied by a teacher, has just arrived for a conducted tour of your large open-plan offices and to see demonstrations of some of the equipment. They have travelled quite a long way by coach and one of the students has been travel sick and feels very unwell. The teacher is reluctant to leave either the group or the sick student. What would you do?

2

The right approach

Precision of communication is important, more important than ever, in our era of hair-trigger balances, when a false or misunderstood word may create as much disaster as a thoughtless act.

JAMES THURBER (1961)

If you have worked your way through the first chapter in this book you should be feeling more aware of the effects personality can have on your working life and the way in which relationships can be maintained or destroyed through a lack of understanding and appreciation of other people.

Getting on with people means communicating, so now let us take a look at the considerations that should be given to the different ways of communicating in the office.

Many years ago, before telephones were a standard item of equipment in most homes, the receipt of a telegram immediately caused anxiety, even before the contents were known. Inland telegrams are not used at all nowadays but, nevertheless, emotions can be aroused by other means:

- A long-awaited telephone call may cause the heart to lurch.
- An envelope marked PRIVATE AND CONFIDENTIAL or PERSONAL could evoke curiosity and, perhaps, concern (if it is addressed to you personally).
- Letters from the Inland Revenue usually cause groans and apprehension!
- A notice on display stating that a certain number of employees are to be made redundant causes shock and a considerable amount of speculation, which can, in turn, promote bitterness and ill-feeling.

Communication media

Throughout your course you will be asked to compose, type, or enact the various means of communicating information, and you will almost certainly pay more attention to *what* you have to say than to *how* you will say it.

When deciding on the 'how' there are two factors to be taken into consideration:

1. The communication medium you will choose to convey this information.
2. The actual words you will use to express your thoughts.

First of all, let us consider some of the communication media that are commonly used in business:

Letter	*Memo*	*Notice*	*Poster*
Report	*Telex*	*Fax*	*Telephone*
Face-to-face	*House magazine*		

The fact that so many different forms exist indicates that each has its own special merits, uses, and effects but is it simply a matter of 'letters are long and used externally, memos are short and used internally'?

The medium chosen will depend on many factors, not least of which are:

- Will the chosen communication medium have the desired effect?
- Is the information being conveyed in the right key?

Getting it right

The straightforward communication of facts creates little problem for the originator, provided they can be set out in a concise and logical fashion, but how often does one convey *just* facts? Even a telex can have a greeting and a short complimentary close!

More frequently, facts have to be couched in the right terms and presented in the most appropriate way in order to have the desired effect.

Before trying to communicate you should try to establish if there is a need for:

- Tact and diplomacy
- A respect for the recipient's feelings
- Persuasion
- Sympathy
- Rebuke

- Privacy
- The creation of a good impression
- Placation
- Motivation
- Amusement

Making the compromise

Once the above has been considered, other factors must also be taken into account before a final decision as to what is the right approach in a given situation can be made:

Urgency   Security   Economy   Record   Facilities available

You may never have considered the importance of these points before, but 'It's not what you say, it's the way that you say it!' that creates the desired effect. If this were not so, would the world give such acclaim to poets and their work?

15

Do you know?
1. The various categories of letters, memos, and reports used in business?
2. What you would expect to find in your company's house journal?
3. Your own word power capability?
4. The different effects that can be created when making face-to-face or telephonic contact?

Snippets
1. Marketing experts recognize the importance of 'personalized' mailing shots and this is greatly facilitated using the merge function on a word processor, thus saving time and money.
2. Telex messages can be made more meaningful without necessarily increasing costs by off-line creation on the teleprinter or word processor screen and their subsequent rapid automatic transmission.
3. Documents transmitted by facsimile telegraphy break through language and time barriers and have legal validity.
4. Some fax machines have a scrambling device incorporated for security purposes.
5. British Telecom Bureaufax International Service enables documents to be transmitted and received between UK and an ever-increasing number of countries. This obviates the problems created by non-compatible machines.

Short problems
1. You are secretary to the general manager of an air cargo company and you are on the rota as relief telephonist/receptionist. It is your day for duty and in the middle of lunchtime a call comes through. Unfortunately it is a very bad line and you hear only words that sound like 'Nicolas', 'Roumania', 'Urgent', and 'Hilton Hotel' and then the line goes dead. You wait 15 minutes but no attempt at contact is made. You feel you must investigate to solve the mystery. You check with the reception diary and find that a Mr Nicolescu has an appointment with your Mr Glendenning next week. Mr Glendenning is at lunch with an important client and unlikely to return until about 4 p.m. His secretary has taken half a day's holiday. What would you do?
2. One of your company's long-standing suppliers and a good acquaintance of your boss is waiting in your office. You like the man and usually have a chat with him about everyday affairs. Today, however, he has a complaint to make about the attitude of one of your department's secretaries when on the phone. This is what he has to say: 'By the way, Barbara, I know you're really keen on good telephone technique so I thought I'd mention to you — not that *I* mind of course — but I do feel one of your secretaries needs a bit of help when on the telephone. I have met the girl and she's pleasant enough. It's Mrs Barnes's secretary. She sounds so sullen and uninterested on the phone. It's all "Yes" and "No" — never any conversation. In fact I began to

wonder if she really understood English! The thing is, some people might take offence and it could affect your business.'

Prepare a list of points to discuss with Mrs Barnes's secretary regarding the greater effort that must be made when talking on the phone, together with the reasons.

Suggested solution to problem 1

1. As you clearly heard the word 'Urgent' you feel it is imperative that you investigate immediately.
2. Check the reception index to see if a card exists for Mr Nicolescu using the cross-referencing system to establish the name, address, and telephone number of the company he represents.

If a card is available
Ring the nearest Hilton Hotel, explain the situation, and ask if they have a reservation in the name of Mr Nicolescu or his company and if any contact has been made.

If the local Hilton has no knowledge
1. Ask if they have a central reservations system for all Hiltons. If so, could they carry out a search using the information you have given them. (He may have been telephoning *from* a Hilton rather than *about* a Hilton.)
2. Find out availability of accommodation in preparation.
3. If the result of the search is positive, contact the Hilton where Mr Nicolescu is staying.

If the result of the search is negative
1. Try to make telephonic contact with the company in Roumania, or better still,
2. Telex to avoid any language barriers and bad lines.

If you can find no information in the reception index
1. Find out if any members of Mr Glendenning's staff know anything about the matter.
2. If so, follow the procedure above.

If no further information is available
1. You can do nothing but await Mr Glendenning's return.
2. Prepare a full message for him.

17

Suggested solution to problem 2

1. Set up a meeting with Mrs Barnes's secretary on neutral ground, say, over coffee. This will prevent her from putting up defence barriers.

2. Broach the subject gently but in a forthright manner with all the facts in your head.

3. Complete deflation can be avoided by emphasizing that the person who has complained has found her pleasant on a face-to-face basis.

4. Ask her for her views about using the telephone. Has she any phobias in this direction?

5. Is using the telephone new to her?

6. Explain the difference between talking to someone face-to-face and to someone on the telephone — no visual image.

7. Explain that she must be able to put a lot more feeling into her voice — 'smile with your voice'.

8. Explain that she must be able to make more than monosyllabic replies — is she afraid to make decisions or suggestions on the telephone?

9. Make her receptive to the idea of telephone training.

Long problem

Ten car parking spaces hitherto allocated to some of the staff are to be reserved for visitors in future and substitute spaces in a less convenient area will be offered to the staff. Discuss possible ways of notifying the staff displaced (e.g., memo, notice, etc.) and say which you think would be most suitable. (LCC PSC)

Suggested approach

For the purpose of this problem, let us assume the following:

1. The staff involved are not top management.

2. Ten specific members of staff are to lose their allocated space (as opposed to the general car park being reduced by 10 spaces).

A change, as indicated in the question, could be construed as lowering the status of the 10 people involved and therefore very careful thought should be given to the communication medium used.

The question only indicates two possible ways of notifying staff. There are in fact several other possibilities. *List them before reading on.*

Memo   Letter   Face-to-face   Notice   Telephonic contact

Could any of these methods be discounted?
We feel that a general notice should be discounted because, while it is quick and cheap, it is a totally impersonal means of conveying information and in this situation could easily create bad feeling. There is no doubt that it needs some careful and diplomatic handling and a notice on this subject would be discourteous, not private, dictatorial, and, in any case, may be overlooked.

Consider the remaining media
Cover up the whole of the Table 2.1 on page 20 except the column headed 'Medium' and develop your answer from the keyword given in this column.

One step further
Would your approach have been any different if you had had to convey 'good' news — for example, informing 10 people that they had been promoted to section leader?

Case study
Tudite is a manufacturer of batteries for both cars and electrically-operated vehicles, such as milk floats. It has two large plants, one in Newcastle and the other in Macclesfield. In addition, there are distribution depots scattered throughout the country in Glasgow, Dundee, Carlisle, Scunthorpe, Wrexham, Ipswich, Halesowen, Portsmouth, and Truro. In all there are some 3000 employees.

This year is the company's Silver Jubilee and as part of the celebrations your boss, Mrs Furness, the public relations officer, would like to revive the house magazine that died a natural death some five years ago. Needless to say the board of directors must be consulted and a great deal of work must be done before its publication. She therefore asks for your assistance and wants you to undertake the following tasks:

1. Draft a memo to the chairman of the company selling the idea of reviving the house magazine.
2. List your thoughts on what information the magazine could contain.
3. Set out a procedure for the creation, collection, editing, and production of the information in its final form.

Table 2.1

Medium	Form	Advantages	Disadvantages	Common Factors
Memo	Open cover	Economical	Impersonal Not private	Ad. Written record Disad. Could be terse Peremptory Produce series of correspondence Gives no prior warning
	Sealed	Confidential		
Letter	Circular	Quicker) than individual Cheaper) letter if no processor	Not personally addressed	Ad. Tone more personal than memo Possibly more detailed than memo Written record Disad. No facility for discussion No prior warning
	Individual	Private Tone more personal Can present individual case	Time-consuming, if no word processor	
Telephone	—	Personal Room for explanation and discussion	May start the grapevine - speculation and resentment No visual image - statements can be misconstrued Time-consuming Possible arguments and bad feeling	
Face to Face	Individual	Personal Enlist support	Time-consuming Grapevine syndrome	Ad. Visual image - seeing reactions aids understanding Explanations possible Disad. Open to argument
	Group	Economic time-wise Person-to-person (as opposed to personal)	Could become emotive More difficult to enlist support Time-consuming if argument ensues	

CONSIDER: Would a combination of any of these methods be suitable? Why?

20

Suggested approach

Draft a memo to the chairman of the company selling the idea of reviving the house magazine

If you are endeavouring to sell, then it is most important that the words, expression, and tone are right, in order to promote favourable thought. Disadvantages should be presented but in a discreet way and strategically placed so as not to dampen enthusiasm.

Answer the following questions in order to gather ideas to present to the chairman of the company:

1. Why might the previous house magazine have died?
2. What are the benefits to the company of having such a publication?
3. What are the benefits to the employees of having such a publication?

Possible disadvantages could be in the areas of:

Cost   *Manning*   *Production*   *Distribution*

Make your own assumptions regarding the company's facilities (here is a good opportunity to revise the various reprographic procedures) and consider ways in which the above factors could be presented to the board in an encouraging way.

Our suggestions appear in Fig. 2.1 on page 22.

List your thoughts on what information the magazine could contain
- Try to obtain a selection of house magazines and study these to gain an overall impression.
- Refer to Fig. 2.1 where the objectives of the magazine are given under points 2 and 3. Look at how these objectives could be achieved in terms of contributions to the magazine.

Our list of suggestions appears below but you should try and produce your own list before reading on.

Social
- Long service employees and presentations.
- Births, engagements, marriages, and deaths.
- Company sports events and achievements.
- Personal achievements including exam successes.
- Clubs, meetings, and outings.
- Welfare services — sickness, retirement.

Creative
- Articles, poetry, anecdotes, cartoons, short stories.
- Hobbies page.
- Crossword and other competitions.

Information
- Items for sale and wanted.
- Holiday information and tips.
- Local events.

1. *Why might the previous house magazine have died?*
- Lack of contributions.
- No fixed procedure for gathering information over a widespread site.
- Editorial and production personnel with insufficient time.
- Lack of variety in contributions and stale presentation.
- Drop in readership.
- May have tried too hard to 'educate' the workers.

2. *What are the benefits to the company of having such a publication?*
- Prestige.
- Coordination between branches.
- The beneficial effect on the employees has a resultant effect on the company's name.
- Makes the company as a corporate body appear more human.
- Important communications medium between the company and its employees.

3. *What are the benefits to the employees of having such a publication?*
- Should foster team-spirit, sense of belonging, company loyalty, solidarity.
- Has the effect of making each employee feel that he can contribute and is not just a number.
- Morale booster.
- Develops friendly rivalry between branches and between departments.
- Encourages the social side of the company to keep going.
- Can present a cheap form of advertising for employees.
- Can provide a vehicle for employees' creative ideas and abilities.

4. *Other considerations*
- Cost is going to be influenced by frequency of publication and the manpower needed to produce and distribute the magazine.
- Suggest an introductory edition to coincide with the date of the company's Silver Jubilee, to be followed by, say, five monthly editions: these trial publications could be undertaken by the public relations staff with the help of temporary staff, as and when needed.
- Cost will also be affected by on-site or off-site printing and the use or non-use of colour and photographs.
- If the magazine's revival is successful, consideration should be given to employing full-time editorial staff and an appropriate allocation should be provided in the company's budget.
- Some of the cost of producing the magazine may be covered by revenue from local advertisers.
- Distribution could be through the channels in use on a daily basis.

Figure 2.1   The objectives of the magazine

	- Letters to the editor (including suggestions on any aspect of the company).
Company news	- Training schemes.
	- Promotions.
	- Welcome notices for executive staff.
	- Sales achievements.
	- New products.

- Articles on company expansion.
- Incentives.

Photographs are vitally important because they add a sense of reality to names.

Silver jubilee edition - History of the firm: premises, product development, number of employees.
- Future aims of the company.
- Jubilee celebrations.
- Stimulate interest in reviving magazine and request for opinions/contributions.

Set out a procedure for the creation, collection, editing, and production of the information in its final form
Below are the problems that are likely to be encountered at each stage. You should consider each one of them and then devise a means of combatting each one. This will then provide you with the outline of a procedure.

Creation
- Stimulate interest and ideas.
- Prior warning if photography needed.
- Insufficient editorial representation throughout the company.

Collection
- Failure to meet deadline dates because of inefficient collection scheduling.

Editing
- Sorting into categories.
- Selection of suitable material:
  • Is it current?
  • Does it need very much editing?
  • Is it the right length?
  • Has it got general appeal?
  • Is it factually correct?

Production
- Putting into a suitable form for printing.
- Sorting page order and page quantity.
- Balancing the display.
- Prevention of errors.
- Production and distribution on time.

One step further

The board of directors has asked Mrs Furness to put forward some suggestions for events to celebrate the Silver Jubilee. Give her some ideas that would be good for the company and some that could be enjoyed by the employees.

Additional problems

1. On your return from lunch an annoyed customer telephones to complain that she is still awaiting a detailed reply — promised over a week ago — to her letter to your employer (who went off on a fortnight's holiday two days ago). She is annoyed still further because she could get no answer from your extension during the last hour.
   (a) What would you say to the customer?
   (b) What would you do?
   (c) How could you prevent a similar situation occurring again?

2. Using an A-Z map of London direct someone from Covent Garden to Horse Guards Parade. Compare the value of giving verbal, written, or graphic directions.

3. Your employer, the sales manager of your company, is in America on a two-week visit. You receive a very strong letter of complaint from a customer stating that a large order that had been promised for a certain date has not been delivered. The customer also states that your area representative knew the order was of great importance to the company. What action would you take? Draft any communications you would write in this connection. (LCC PSC)

Part Two

The importance of good planning

3

Are you sitting comfortably?

It's a pity to shoot the pianist when the piano is out of tune.
RENE COTY (1957)

'Is there anything else you would like to know about the job?' the interviewer said.

'Yes, please!' replied the potential secretary. 'What sort of typewriter will I have to use?'

There is no doubt that the above is one of the most overworked questions used by secretaries when undergoing an interview — yet is the typewriter the only factor that causes concern when talking about the office environment in which you are going to spend about one-third of your working day? The best typewriters in the world would not ensure good work if:

- The area in which you had to work resembled Paddington station at rush hour.
- You had to do a 100-metre dash to the nearest toilets.
- The desks and chairs looked as if they had been bought from a museum.
- You got stuck to the typing chair every time you sat on it.
- The colour of the paint depressed you!

Are you sitting comfortably?

While your effectiveness in your job will depend to a large degree on your own particular skills and expertise, the human body still functions better in surroundings that are conducive to the work being undertaken, and this has for many years been the subject of study, experiment, and legislation. We are talking here, not only of the physical comforts of the worker but also the mental comforts — the creation of a clear and peaceful mind, receptive to the tasks of the day. There is a definite 'grey' area where the physical aspects ultimately affect the mental attitude.

As a result of the studies and experiments that have been undertaken, office design and planning consultants exist to ensure that the available space is used to the best possible advantage, taking into consideration the particular functional relationships involved and adhering to the requirements of the law, the available light, and the outlook.

Physical factors that affect performance

A great many people suffer from backache and this is aggravated by sitting in chairs that do not give adequate support or leaning over tables and desks that are too high or too low.

Furniture
- Tables and desks of stipulated minimum height.
- Chairs designed to ensure correct lumbar support.
- Typists' chairs adjustable for angle and height of back support and angle of seat.
- Cabinets within reach or with the provision of a safe means of elevation.
- Avoidance of surfaces that reflect light and cause glare.
- Use of screens to provide a degree of privacy.
- Use of screens for VDU work.

Heating
The law recognizes a minimum level below which efficiency is affected. Yet over-heated offices (whether by artificial or natural means) can cause efficiency to be drastically reduced through both bodily and mental discomforts.

Ventilation
While the law does make stipulations regarding the amount of ventilation, what may be 'adequate' for one person at a specific time, doing a specific job may be totally inadequate for another doing a completely different task.

Lighting
Fluorescent fittings give a more even distribution of light but can cause monotony and visual fatigue. The flickering, faulty tube can also be a grave distraction.

Noise
Can be broken down into:

1. *Machine noise:* typewriters, printers, telex, telephones, photocopiers, etc. This can be alleviated by the use of hoods and baffler screens, 'trimphones' and lights instead of bells.
2. *Occupational noise:* level of voices, movement of people, and paper. This can be alleviated by the use of screens, acoustic ceilings, carpets, curtains, wall coverings for sound absorbency, the creation of good workflow to minimize movement, and the use of masking to override noise in an open-plan environment.
3. *Extraneous noise:* traffic, pneumatic drills, plant, and machinery. This can be alleviated by the use of double-glazing.

Colour
Colour can affect the moods of the occupants of the room in which it is used. Colours should be chosen to reflect light, to give a feeling of space, to brighten dark corners, and to create a restful atmosphere.

Decor
The facility for employees to decorate their own working area with appropriate plants, pictures, and wall hangings helps to avoid the impersonal atmosphere so predominant in well-planned, well-organized offices.

The intangibles that affect performance
While outside worries may, to some degree, affect our working lives, discomfort and stress may be caused in the working situation in ways that are not immediately obvious to the sufferer especially if he or she appears to be the only one affected.

We need to analyse our feelings and try to pinpoint the causes. Feelings of insecurity, of uncertainty, of frustration, of resentment, of anxiety, of listlessness, and of being disorganized all cause tension but some, at least in the working situation, could be lessened.

Job security Awareness of company progress; awareness of one's own security of employment (matter of self-respect); confidence in having sickness pay, holiday pay; provision of some flexibility in the working day, i.e., flexitime, thus allowing for the unexpected appointment; adequate salary.

Job satisfaction Job exercising one's capabilities but not beyond them; scope clearly delineated in job specification — status clearly defined; degree of responsibility clarified; promotion prospects.

Isolation Engendered by some jobs needing concentrated attention, i.e., audio-typists, word processing operators; provision needed for rest periods and for a room in which to relax.

Can you affect your own performance?

In some ways this introduction has come full circle, because, even given the best working environment in the world, you will not be guaranteed to produce good work at a good rate if your particular organizing skills are limited. A tidy approach to work does help to develop a tidy mind so before continuing through this chapter, analyse your own particular method of working.

Do you know?
1. The requirements of the Health and Safety at Work Act with regard to space, lighting, ventilation, heating, and toilet and cloakroom facilities?
2. How open-plan and landscaped offices differ and how they evolved?
3. The measurements recommended by The British Standards Institution for typists' desks and chairs?
4. That ergonomics has been defined as the 'anatomical, physiological, and psychological study of man in his working environment'?

Snippets
1. An office chair has been marketed that can be completely adjusted from the sitting position. The correct and most comfortable position is recorded on a digital display. A change in posture causes the seat to shift — this helps to stimulate muscular activity and blood circulation in the legs.
2. BS5252 1976 provides colour coordination for building purposes — specific ranges may be chosen from 237 systematically-related colours.
3. A new electronic air conditioning system decontaminates and deodorizes air conditioning ducts and prevents re-circulation of polluted air.
4. Energy management systems are programmed to control heating and air conditioning systems at maximum efficiency and conserve energy at the same time. An optimal-start controller will turn on the heating system just before it is required: zone controllers — microprocessor-based — control up to five devices in different zones. More sophisticated systems monitor and control energy consumption in the building and react to people and equipment heat emission.
5. The Disabled Persons (Employment) Acts 1944 and 1958 place the obligation upon employers with 20 or more workers to give employment to registered

disabled up to a quota, that is a proportion of their total staff. The standard
percentage is at present 3 per cent.
6. Loughborough University VDU Eye Test Advisory Group has drawn up a package
of tests particularly relevant to VDU operators.

Short problems

1. It is the first job your junior has ever had and while you feel she is basically
capable, she seems to work in a constant muddle and this leads to uncorrec-
ted mistakes and delays in the production of work. How could you suggest
she might improve and thus make life easier for herself?
2. You work for the production manager of a firm producing novelty goods
and you are recruiting more assembly workers because the busiest time of
the year is fast approaching. The personnel manager has just phoned you to
say that she has, this morning, interviewed 10 applicants, 7 of whom seem to
be highly suitable. She explains that there may, however, be a problem with
one of them because she is confined to a wheelchair. The personnel manager
is very keen to employ her because she has demonstrated a high degree of
dexterity and asks you to investigate any problems that may arise.

Suggested solution to problem 1

1. Ensure a good start to the day — prompt arrival.
2. Maintain basic tidiness: in your person, in your handbag (avoid rummag-
ing for keys, pens, etc.), and your shopping bags; clothes should be put in
the place provided and the typewriter cover folded away.
3. Drawer tidiness — a place for everything — pens, rubbers, paper, carbons,
keep everything in its place; label drawers.
4. Best use of available space, e.g., modular furniture — flexibility in using
available surfaces to suit particular requirements, such as collating on long
surfaces, moving machinery as necessary.
5. Desk-top tidiness — remove all unnecessary papers and files — use of
baskets. Use containers for paper clips, pins, etc.
6. Working order left to right or right to left — completed work on opposite
side to natural working side.
7. Use of waste paper bin when needed — discard spoilt sheets immediately
— avoids searching for 'best' copies.
8. Be prepared : notepad for phone messages; notebooks for dictation,
instructions, callers, lists of jobs, and priorities.
9. Put things away when a job is completed and before starting another.
10. At the end of the day, completely clear the desk, putting everything away
in its proper place. This ensures a good start to the next day.

Suggested solution to problem 2
Your investigations

1. Can she get to the production department? Is the goods lift capable of taking a wheelchair?

2. Are the corridors wide enough to negotiate?

3. Are the doorways to be used wide enough?

4. Is there sufficient manoeuvrability in the workspace — is all work within reach?

5. Are there any steps to negotiate — need for a ramp?

6. Accessibility of any equipment to be used and stored?

7. Toilet space — need for cubicle reorganization?

8. Are other personnel willing to assist — getting to canteen — picking up dropped articles — fetching new supplies?

Check with personnel officer

1. Can the disabled person:
- Get out of her car and into her wheelchair?
- Manoeuvre herself to use the toilet facilities?
- Carry a cup of tea as well as drive her wheelchair?

2. Is the chair electrically operated?

3. How much will she have to rely on other staff?

Case study

Margaret is employed as secretary to the electrical goods sales manager of a medium-sized mail order company. She works in a large open-plan office (a diagram for which is given in Fig. 3.1) which is heated by a warm air system.

Her single pedestal wooden desk is positioned outside her boss's private office near to the double swing doors that form the main entrance to the office. She operates her own filing system and the cabinets are in the sales manager's office. All employees in the department use the photocopier a great deal and coffee and tea breaks are taken on a staggered rota basis. Every clerk has access to a telephone.

It is her responsibility to sort and distribute the mail for the whole of this department but she works solely for the sales manager. Outgoing mail is placed by individuals on the mail table for collection by the post room messenger.

She has held responsible posts before but this one seems to be beating her. She is finding it extremely difficult to keep up to date with her work, her typing seems to be going to pieces, and she is constantly tired, yet she does not lead a particularly hectic social life.

Identify the possible causes of her difficulties, the effects these are having on her performance, and suggest ways in which they could be realistically resolved.

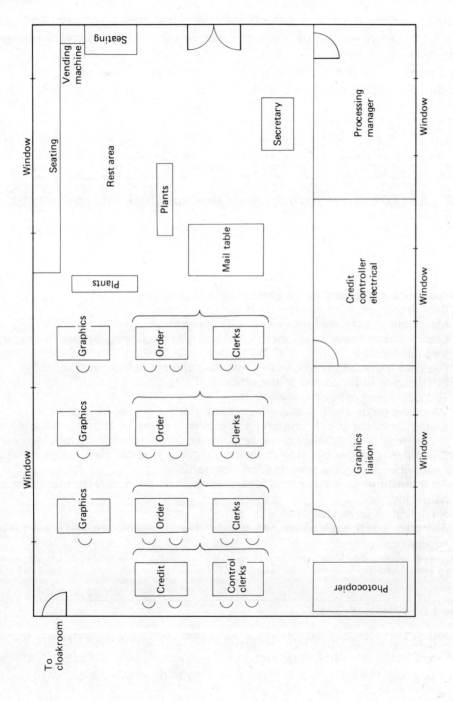

Figure 3.1 Plan of the electrical goods sales department

Suggested approach

To help you to identify the possible causes, do the following exercise and answer the questions.

1. Using different coloured pencils for the clerks, the secretary, and other personnel, work out people's general movement paths. What conclusion do you draw from this?
2. Consider the layout of the office and identify problem areas?
3. Could the positions of the windows and doors be causing her to have problems?
4. Could noise be a contributory factor?
5. Is the routine task she has to undertake likely to cause her any problems?
6. Do you consider her workstation to be suitable?
7. How could her past experience be different from her present job?

Make a list of the causes you have established and check your answers with our suggestions in Fig. 3.2.

---

1. ● Too much movement by all personnel.
2. ● Rest area open to remainder of office.
   ● Mail table — centre of room — untidy appearance.
   ● Clerks' desks badly positioned — necessitates weaving around them to go through far door.
   ● Files not immediately to hand — may sometimes be inaccessible.
   ● Photocopier in far corner of the office.
   ● Thoroughfare past secretary's desk.
3. ● Windows on far wall — away from natural light — may be gloomy.
   ● Swing doors constantly opening and closing — may be causing draughts.
4. ● Noise from: ringing telephones, typewriters, vending machine, photocopier.
   ● Noise from: people chatting in rest area; going past her desk; stopping at her desk; when using the photocopier; generally.
5. ● Time-consuming sorting and distributing mail especially if there are two deliveries.
   ● No provision for sorted mail.
6. ● Secretary's desk badly positioned, unattractive in appearance, and inadequate in capacity.
7. ● May have worked in cellular office — used to privacy or landscaped office — used to refinements.

Figure 3.2 Suggested causes

Study the possible causes of Margaret's difficulties and consider what effects these may have, not only upon her but on other people working in the office.

Think about the following keywords and try to determine if any of the causes would produce any of these effects. You may feel that some of the causes would have the same effects.

- Distracted
- Unable to concentrate
- Worried at her inability to concentrate
- Frustrated
- Annoyed
- Muddled
- Unwell
- Depressed
- Claustrophobic
- Uncomfortable
- Panic stricken
- Disorganized
- Embarrassed
- Fatigued

You have now identified the problems that could be contributing to Margaret's poor performance and tiredness. You now need to consider how the situation may be improved. Look at the following questions and try to answer them noting any suggestions that occur to you.

1. How could the movement of personnel be reduced?
2. How could the desks be regrouped to improve the situation and possibly the workflow?
3. If the mail table was against the wall, how would you improve sorting the mail?
4. Is sorting a specialist job or could anyone else do it?
5. Where could the photocopier be re-sited?
6. Do the files have to be situated in the sales manager's office to be kept securely? What other solutions could you make?
7. What could be achieved by borrowed light, hydraulic closure, and use of colour?
8. What use would baffler screens have in this environment?
9. What other ideas do you have to reduce noise, to help Margaret to organize herself, and to improve the general appearance and the psychological effects of this office?

One step further
If, after the reorganization of the office, Margaret still felt the same, what other possible causes could there be?

Long problem

Your boss, the general manager, has informed you that the company is considering changing the typists' desks and chairs, which are nearly 20 years old, and is thinking of acquiring new furniture that would be more suitable for the screen-based word processors that have recently been installed. Since the installation, there has been a spate of complaints about headaches and back-aches.

The typists have undergone a two-day off-site training course in using the machines and did not make any complaints at that time. There appears to be no resentment or resistance to the system; in fact, the girls seem to be fascinated at what can be done.

The general manager has asked you to list those points you would consider essential in selecting furniture for people working with such equipment. You have also been asked if you can establish some reasons for the complaints.

Suggested approach

It is important to ensure that the old desks and chairs are replaced by appropriate ergonomically-designed furniture to enable the operators to see the keyboard and screen clearly, and position the paper source material correctly.

Assume, for the purposes of this problem, that the equipment which has been installed falls into one of the following categories, and justify your decision:

- A combined drive unit/screen/keyboard.
- A combined screen/keyboard with free-standing drive unit or shared logic system.
- An adjustable pedestal screen, separate keyboard and free-standing drive unit or shared logic system.

Chairs Consider what type of chair is suitable for this kind of work bearing in mind:

- People of different heights.
- People of varying limb sizes.
- People with short arm reaches.
- People with long arm reaches.
- People with different eye heights.

It must be possible for everyone using the machines to make coordinated movements and to use the machine without strain.

Desks Surface area required will depend upon the size of word processor used.

- Is it possible to obtain a desking system that can be raised and is it desirable?
- Are there any advantages in using modular furniture in this situation?
- What are the advantages of having workstations that are fully-wired and fitted with storage facilities?
- What considerations will you give to workflow?

From the points you have gathered, list the recommendations you would make when choosing furniture to be used in this situation.

Backache and headaches may be caused by the old and unsuitable furniture, especially as these did not occur during off-site training when correctly designed furniture was probably used. Could there be other causes that could be remedied?

Although the VDU emits light, light is also reflected by it.

How do you think the equipment should be positioned in relation to:

- Light from low angle sources, such as windows and table lamps?
- Light from bulbs or tubes?
- Reflection from gloss paint, shiny furniture, shiny keys, and mirrors?

Is the fluorescent lighting combining with that of the VDU to produce a stroboscopic effect?

Could the VDU itself be creating problems over a longer period of time in terms of:

- The cursor?
- The colour of the lettering on the screen?
- The instructions on the screen?
- The display being different from the printed page?
- Over-use of the scrolling facility?

How can the company ensure that operators can cope with a visually more demanding job?

Could the position of the printer be having an effect? What would you recommend to reduce these effects?

Given the ideal equipment and conditions, is there any reason why the operators would be tense, which in turn would cause aches?

The following keywords should help you to identify such causes:

Incentives	*Status*	*Work measurement / Production rate*
Overstretching	*Rest*	*Isolation*

37

One step further

If the installation of this equipment had, from the start, caused resentment and resistance, in addition to a spate of headaches and backaches, what other factors could be the cause of this reaction and what remedial measures could be taken?

Additional problems

1. A new reception room is to be set up by your company. Advise the office manager what will be required to ensure that this operates efficiently. (LCC PSC)

2. You have been interviewed for two secretarial positions. The first is Secretary to a Senior Executive in a large organisation where you would work only for that executive and have your own office. The second is Secretary to the Directors of a small family organisation where you would work for the three Directors and the General Manager and share an open-plan office with seven other people.

(a) Explain the differences you would expect to find between the two organisations insofar as they would affect yourself.
(b) State which position you would prefer and briefly explain why. (LCC PSC)

4

At all events

Everybody has his own theatre, in which he is manager, actor, prompter, playwright, sceneshifter, boxkeeper, doorkeeper, all in one, and audience into the bargain.
HARE (1792-1834)

If you have covered the basic principles to be remembered when arranging conferences, you will appreciate the importance, as in all areas of secretarial work, of a systematic approach. Even the smallest detail, if overlooked, could cause inconvenience, embarrassment, and even complete disruption of the proceedings:

The forgotten projector

- The forgotten projector.
- The projector that has not been checked.
- The handicapped delegate who cannot use the toilet facilities.
- The bouquets of flowers left in the ladies' powder room because nobody was asked to present them.
- The slides that are upside down.
- The foreign delegates who do not speak English and no interpreter is available.

All areas must be covered and this includes — in addition to running the conference itself — spouses' programmes, if they are present; the social activities outside conference hours; the administration involved in ensuring that everyone, delegates and presenters alike, have all they require.

Will it affect me?

At this juncture, if you have definite ideas about working for a small company, you may well be thinking that this section is not for you. We can, however, quote the example of the secretary who went to work for a small business. The idea of organizing conferences probably never entered her head. Yet her boss was also a member of a worldwide service organization and he was chosen to organize the annual three-day conference in his town. This required several months of planning in which his secretary was very deeply involved.

On the other hand, you can probably see a much clearer connection between large companies and conferences.

Why hold conferences?

Conferences are held for a variety of reasons but all provide an occasion for people to get out of their working environment and meet on an even footing.

All the participants may be business associates but meeting in neutral surroundings is thought to have very beneficial psychological effects:

- Relaxation.
- Increased feelings of confidence and security.
- Lowering of status and communication barriers.
- Increase in powers of concentration.

These effects can in turn lead to actions that may be very different from the norm:

- Freer expression of views.

- Greater exchange of ideas.
- Willingness to make and renew acquaintances.
- Greater appreciation of other people's problems.
- Greater participation.

By creating such a climate the conference aims of the company are more likely to be realized, and these may include any or all of the following:

- To boost morale.
- To up-date on new technology, new products.
- To demonstrate company prosperity and advancement (unsuccessful companies tend not to hold conferences).
- To increase solidarity, company loyalty, and team spirit.
- To revitalize staff in their approach.
- To introduce and explain new policies or management techniques.

These aims will, however, not be achieved if frustration is engendered by poor organization.

Remember: For the conference organizer even the minutest detail is of paramount importance.

The conferences industry

Over recent years conferences have become more and more sophisticated and this has led to the growth of the conference and exhibitions industry that is made up of thousands of specialists in their own right. It has even developed its own language (e.g., meetings buyers, meetings suppliers, incentives, incentivators). Some of these organizations can take on the arrangements for the event in entirety, others provide a specialist service. You may find a job in such an organization very stimulating.

Press conferences

These obviously have a very different format from the type of company conferences we have just mentioned but nevertheless they involve a certain amount of planning because they are usually held to project an image — product/products/service/company — and hence any secretary involved must give a great deal of care and attention to organizing for the comfort of the press:

- Comfortable seating.
- Provision of refreshments (depending on the time of day).

41

- Smoking facilities.
- Good lighting for photography and filming.
- Sufficient power points.
- Sufficient room for equipment.
- Welcoming procedure and security check.
- Provision of sufficient literature, leaflets, samples, technical, and any other promotional information.
- Presence of experts.

Trade fairs and exhibitions

Many companies, both large and small, promote their products in this way There are exhibition centres all over the world and at any given time there will always be an exhibition in progress somewhere. The organization of stands at trade fairs is an industry in itself and includes contract companies for such things as lighting, carpeting, furnishing, and even cleaning the stands.

Do you know?
1. How you would expect a conference, seminar, and course to differ?
2. How seating arrangements can differ and the psychological effect that these are purported to have?
3. How you would ensure the confidentiality of documents at a conference?
4. What is included in conference packages offered by hotel groups?
5. That certain towns specialize in conference facilities, have a conference officer, and publish their own detailed brochures?
6. That conferences may be political, union, corporate, trade, product launch, educational?

Snippets
1. An 'incentive' is a motivation scheme operated by an 'incentivator'. An incentive must pay for itself — increased sales, profits, energy saving, increased efficiency — otherwise it is simply a perk, an extra holiday, a tax dodge. It should also have a serious conference element.
2. A magazine is published monthly called *Conferences and Exhibitions International* which contains a wealth of information for anyone planning such an event.
3. A number of universities and polytechnics offer conference facilities during the Easter, summer, and Christmas vacations.
4. British Rail offer an inter-city exhibitions train service in conjunction with private enterprise contractors. This can include a cinema, bar, and lounge facilities and enables a daily change of venue. It is possible to exhibit abroad in this way.
5. A British exhibitions promotion council has been formed whose main task is 'to promote, project, and protect UK-based exhibitions and British participation overseas'.
6. A company called Exp-O-Tel produces booklets for all major exhibitions giving a selection of good hotels that offer accommodation at special rates for exhibitors and visitors. They also offer a centralized booking service.

Short problems

1. Your employer, an accountant, is the 'speaker finder' for his club and has booked a well-known, interesting, and amusing TV personality who is willing to spend an evening giving a talk for local charities. You have had 150 tickets printed and have booked a suitable room in a good hotel with a large car park and arranged for bar facilities in the room and a buffet to take place at the end of the talk. All the tickets have been sold and requests are still coming in!

On the afternoon of the talk, when your employer is out with a client until 4 p.m., you receive a telephone call from the hotel manager who tells you that a pipe has burst and the room booked for the talk is under water and will be out of use for several days. She offers you an alternative room but insists that this will only hold 120 people. (She is adamant that no more than the stipulated number can be accommodated because of fire regulations). How would you deal with this situation?

2. You are secretary to the sales director of a small but expanding hardware manufacturing company currently selling in the southern counties of England. The board of directors has decided that in the next stage of development they would like national sales coverage and, if possible, overseas sales distribution, for their range of products. As the sales director is an extremely busy man he has asked you to investigate what is involved in taking a trade stand at an appropriate exhibition in the UK. A total budget of £8000 will be available including accommodation for four of the company's own staff.

Suggested solution to problem 1

It would not be possible to change the venue:

- Had another hotel in the same group been available, the manager would already have made enquiries.
- It would be impossible to change to a hall because of the buffet, bar, and other facilities that would be required.
- A change of venue would necessitate changing the time of the talk and diverting a large number of people and cars.
- A complete change of hotel would not be possible in a small town and in any case it would be extremely short notice to produce a buffet for 150 people.

A compromise solution must therefore be found in the hotel booked.

1. Is there a small room, preferably in close proximity to the one offered, which can seat 30 people?

2. Can the smaller room be wired up for sound and vision?

3. Are there bar facilities both in the large and small rooms offered and, if not, could they be provided?

4. When the talk ends could the chairs be stacked away quickly in the large room so that all can participate in the buffet and meet the speaker?

Assuming that the manager says that closed circuit television (CCTV) is viable:

5. Contact the television engineering company and explain the circumstances. Try to negotiate favourable terms especially as the event is for charity.

6. Ring the hotel manager, and explain the arrangements made for CCTV installation.

7. When your employer returns at 4 o'clock, tell him what you have done. He may decide to telephone some of his club members to give them advance warning of the new arrangement. It should be possible to find 30 'volunteers' to sit in the smaller room — a small refund should be offered to those inconvenienced.

8. Ensure that someone (you, your boss, or another club member) checks up on the new arrangements and is present to greet the guests.

9. Ascertain that the manager of the hotel has provided direction signs to the additional room.

Suggested solution to problem 2

1. Study the hardware trade journals and determine dates and venues of fairs in the UK. The term 'international' usually indicates that the fair will be a large one attended by foreign buyers.

2. Write to organizers of fairs — for example, at the National Exhibition Centre, Birmingham; Olympia or Earl's Court, London; the Royal Highland Exhibition Centre, near Edinburgh. Ascertain the space available, the types of stand offered (i.e., space only or purpose-built with walls and flooring), and the price per square metre. Request a plan of the halls to locate the position of available stands. Ask when the deposit is required and what the payment arrangements are.

3. Write to the hardware trade journals to obtain attendance figures of home retail and wholesale buyers, number of overseas buyers attending, and countries represented. Request the advertising cost for a pre-exhibition advertisement, which should inform clients and potential buyers of the location of the stand at the exhibition.

4. Organizers should forward not only details of space and prices but also information on contractors to prepare the stand: e.g., electrical companies for lighting and power points; stand-fitting companies for on-stand display fixtures. Written quotes should then be obtained from these.

5. Obtain the cost of daily cleaning of the stand from cleaning companies and the cost of floral displays.

6. Contact Exp-O-Tel for hotel accommodation. (Send for the booklet if not received from the fair organizers.)
7. Obtain the cost of preparing publicity material including price lists — provide for a batch to go to the press office of the fair centre.
8. Assess the appropriate subsistence allowance for company representatives.
9. Obtain quotes, or discuss with the transport department, the cost of carrying products and other equipment to and from the fair.
10. Report on findings — allow a figure in the budget for give-aways.

Long problem

You work for a publishing company that specializes in business books. Every year a three-day conference is run for practising teachers. This event is usually held during July using a university campus.

Several speakers are engaged to talk on their specialisms and these talks are interspersed with workshop sessions run by experts. On one evening there is a formal meal and the other two evenings are organized on an informal basis.

You have been asked to head the team organizing the conference. List the tasks that need to be undertaken and identify how you would carry out each effectively.

Suggested approach

Figure 4.1 shows the three aspects of conference organization that must be dealt with in order to achieve success.

A flowchart is given for each aspect (Figs 4.2, 4.3, 4.4), which you should work through, trying to anticipate each step before referring to it.

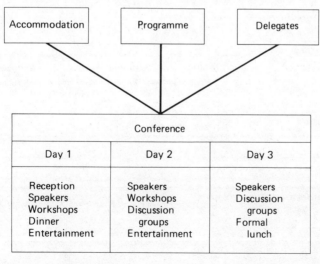

Figure 4.1 Flowchart showing the three main aspects of conference organization

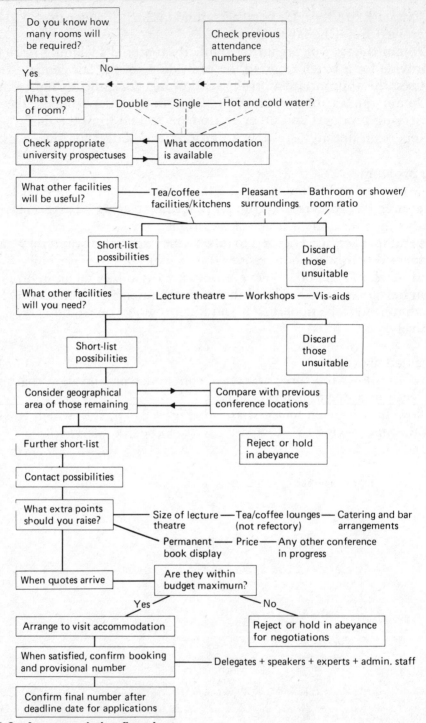

Figure 4.2 Accommodation flowchart

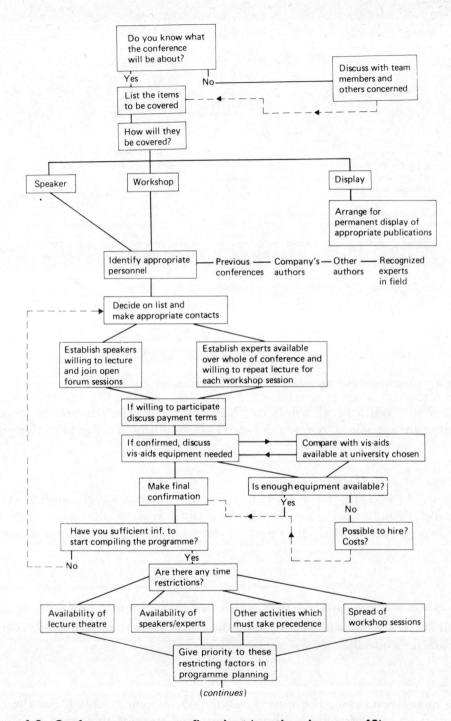

Figure 4.3 Conference programme flowchart (*continued on page 48*)

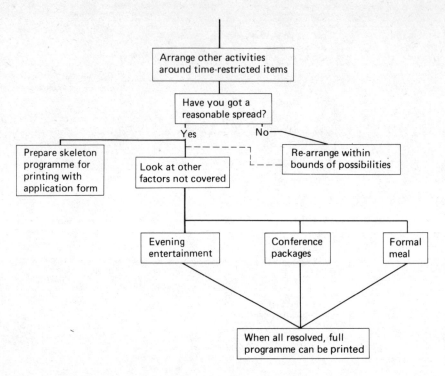

Figure 4.3 Conference programme flowchart (*continued*)

There are still several points to be settled before the conference begins. Consider the questions given under each side heading in order to evolve your answer.

Evening entertainment
What would you suggest as on-campus entertainment for one night? What might be a suitable outing for the second evening? How would you arrange this so that delegates could decide after arrival? Have you thought about transport?

Conference packages
Will delegates need some form of identification? Is a better impression made if handouts and details are presented in one file? What other information could the package contain?

Formal meal
What sort of menu could the university offer? What about staffing? Are there to be any guest speakers? If so, what do you need to do with regard to:

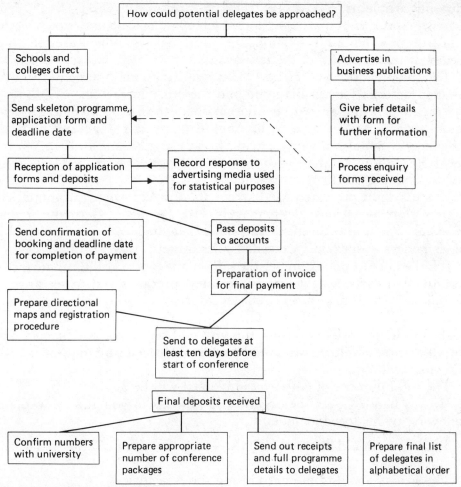

Figure 4.4 Delegates' flowchart

- Accommodation?
- Topic of talk?
- Formal presentation?
- Vote of thanks?

What do you need to do about seating arrangements? Can the catering services at the university provide the ancillary services such as flower arrangements, menu printing, and wine service?

One step further

You are now ready for the conference to take place but the work of any organizer does not end there. What jobs will you have to undertake immediately prior to, during, and after the conference?

Additional problems

1. Lorenzo SpA is an Italian company which manufactures and exports Italian fine art reproductions throughout the world. Their products are very much aimed at the 'top end' of the market.

The main factory and Head Office is in Milan and there are two other smaller factories, one in Bergamo and the other in Brescia.

You are personal assistant to Giorgio Blake, the European Sales Director, based in Milan. Mr Blake is of Anglo-Italian parentage and he speaks French and Spanish fluently, in addition to English and Italian. You also speak English and Italian with some knowledge of German. Most of your correspondence to clients is in English.

You have just presented Mr Blake with a breakdown of the annual sales figures from the various sales managers (UK, Denmark, Germany, France, Holland, Spain and Sweden) and he is delighted with the results which have, generally speaking, exceeded sales targets.

It is the normal procedure for the sales managers to visit the main factory in Milan in early May to view the latest products and to see any new techniques which may have been developed.

In recognition of the efforts made by all the European field sales staff, Mr Blake would like you to combine this visit with a seminar and incentive trip for all of these employees and their partners. He feels sure that the board of directors will agree.

The total number of employees involved will be 38.

He has handed over the organization of this to you and he wants the following points to be included:

- 3 full days should be spent in Italy — i.e., the whole of Friday, Saturday and Sunday.
- The Friday should be spent visiting the 3 factories.
- A half-day seminar will take place on the Saturday morning at the Company's Head Office in their board room. This will consist of a talk by the company's industrial psychologist, Signor Giovanni Lessini, on psychology in selling and developing effective communication patterns. Mr Blake will also give a talk on modern sales techniques and the art of creative selling. Each of the sales managers in the group will be required to give a five-minute talk on experiences in his particular area. There will also be an Open Forum session.
- The remainder of the weekend can be spent at Stresa on Lake Maggiore. Each country will have to make the necessary travelling arrangements to and from Milan but the internal group travel arrangements will be made by you.

List the tasks that have to be done using the following guidelines:

- Appropriate accommodation.
- Visits to the factories.
- Half-day seminar.
- Plans for the partners when the employees are occupied.
- Investigate entertainment and excursion possibilities in Stresa.
- Organize a formal dinner for the Sunday evening.

2. COMPUTELL LIMITED a UK-owned and registered company, which has been involved for some years in the manufacturing and marketing of computer hardware, will shortly be entering the market as a distributor of American-manufactured computer units for use in the home and within the price range of £600 - £3,000. It is expected that the equipment will be used by business people based in their homes, by professional persons, as well as for educational and various house-hold purposes. The plans are for a phased introduction, both geographically (to cover, eventually, most parts of the UK) and by range of products. Selling will be by direct contact with potential purchasers and users among the general public as well as by dealings through the trade. The existing sales staff (experienced only in the selling of equipment to industrial and commercial users) will in part be used, together with additional personnel already being recruited especially for the new domestic selling market.

The Company intends holding a two-day residential conference of area managers and sales representatives, to be held in The Supreme Hotel at Harrogate. The aims of the conference will be to outline the marketing objectives of the company, to explain the new sales system, to describe the changes in consumer legislation in recent years and to discuss the implications thereof and to act as a preliminary to forthcoming detailed technical training. Part of the programme will be an open forum to which members of the technical press will be invited.

You are required to devise a programme for the conference in a form suitable for the issue to the relevant employees. You should include in the programme any matters, in addition to those mentioned above, that you consider would be appropriate. (RSA PA DIP)

Meetings are a little more than terminology

You have displaced the mirth, broke the good meeting, with most admir'd disorder.

SHAKESPEARE (1564-1616)

You will now have learned the basic theory of meetings and committee procedure and you may well be struggling to learn a list of terms used in connection with such meetings. It is also hoped that you will have had the opportunity of typing the various documents used in connection with meetings and have gained an understanding of the sequencing of such documents.

In spite of the rather glamorous idea of meetings, there may in fact be a great deal of frustration and boredom. Indeed, some such gatherings consist mainly of lengthy irrelevant discussion which ultimately leads nowhere, accomplishes very little, and results in a fall in the numbers of people who subsequently attend. As a policy-making body it is then neither representative nor effective.

Your role in formal meetings

Have you considered how your job will differ as secretary to the chairman of a committee; as secretary to the secretary of a committee; or even as the committee secretary yourself?

Did you know that as either secretary to the committee chairman *or* the committee secretary it may be your job to take the minutes of the meeting? In addition, as secretary to the chairman you could be concerned with assisting him in his role of running the meeting efficiently by having the right documents to hand when needed; ensuring that follow-up action is noted; and, once the meeting is over, that it is in fact 'followed up'.

As secretary to the committee secretary, on the other hand, your involvement may be even greater. The secretary's role entails a great deal of the 'donkey work' needed in the planning and preparation of meetings. You will,

Meetings are a little more than terminology

therefore, be concerned not only with typing meetings documents but also with the other work that has to be carried out prior to final arrangements being made. These jobs may include contacting members for suggestions before an agenda is drafted; organizing the room (reservation, seating, heating, lighting, spare agendas, stationery, attendance record); organizing refreshments (including the provision of water carafes); possibly reading the minutes (if these have not already been circulated); taking the minutes, drafting and circulating them; and taking any follow-up action.

If, however, you take on the responsibility of committee secretary, you would still be required to ensure that all the above tasks are carried out, but in this instance your role may change from you actually doing the jobs to having the jobs done for you.

If, on the other hand, you are involved in the arrangements for the annual general meeting of your company, you will find that preparations have to be made on a much grander scale, from the notice in the press to refreshments for a large number of people.

53

Informal meetings — are they still a matter of good planning?

The need for advanced planning and for an organized procedure at formal meetings is probably obvious to you, especially if you have attended a formal meeting, such as that of a local council. You may also have seen a John Cleese film of how *not* to run a meeting: no agenda — no procedure — no control and no action!

But do you consider that it is necessary to plan for an informal meeting and especially if this is held in the office of your boss and is composed of a group of people having an informal discussion or a brainstorming session?

Can you, in fact, hold any kind of meeting without some kind of organized structure?

How will you, as your boss's secretary, call the meeting?

Memos?   *Telephone calls?*   *Face-to-Face?*

However you contact the people your boss wants to attend, you must have a list of names, addresses and telephone numbers, together with a system of noting those who have been contacted and those who have agreed to come. It may be that the meeting won't be held unless some particular person or persons are definitely able to attend.

Even for informal brainstorming sessions you must still ensure the availability of the room or, if your boss's office is to be used, that his diary is clear and that there will be no interruptions. Make sure also that the room is properly prepared with sufficient chairs, ashtrays, writing paper, space, and implements and that the heating and ventilation is appropriately adjusted. Arrangements must also be made for the provision of refreshments — it could be a very vocal and thirsty session!

Your boss will have called the meeting for a specific purpose, yet the agenda may contain only the briefest details. It is, therefore, vitally important that you ensure that he enters the meeting well prepared with all the files and documents he may require.

In addition, your boss may want you to take notes rather than minutes for subsequent leisurely study. Therefore you must ensure that you are knowledgeable about the topics to be discussed and that your office is manned to cope with callers and telephone calls in your absence to avoid unnecessary interruptions.

It can, therefore, be seen that even with informal meetings there is a degree of planning, of attention to detail, and, on your part as secretary, of involvement.

Do you know?
1. The meaning of such terms as:
   - Go into committee?

- Point of order?
- Lie on the table?
- Standing orders?
- Minutes of narration?

2. The difference between, for example:
   - A motion carried unanimously and a motion carried *nem con?*
   - Adjournment and postponement?
   - Coopted member and *ex officio* member?
   - Amendment and rider?
   - Agenda and chairman's agenda?
   - A formal and informal meeting?

3. That for a meeting to be valid it must be:
   - Properly constituted?
   - Properly convened?
   - Properly conducted?

On the other hand, a properly organized meeting with a firm chairman who keeps discussion to the point at issue and ensures that decisions are reached by majority agreement, after everyone entitled to do so has expressed their views, should be effective and achieve the objectives of the meeting.

4. Which standard items should appear on the agenda for an AGM:
   - For a limited liability company?
   - For a social organization?

Snippets

1. In the meeting room, put place names in position and prepare a plan of the seating arrangements. This will help you to identify the speakers and so aid minute taking.
2. When typing up the minutes you must differentiate between the members of the board or committee (these are said to be *present*) and those people who have attended by invitation, perhaps to give advice, or simply in a working capacity, such as the minute secretary (these are said to be *in attendance*).
3. Look at the rules and regulations governing the meeting body to check whether *ex officio* and coopted members have voting rights. This will also help to decide whether the latter whould appear as present or in attendance.
4. When preparing for an AGM consider the total number of members concerned and the need to prepare proxy forms to accompany the agenda and voting papers for the election of officials at the meeting itself.

Short problems

1. Is there any difference between a meeting that has been postponed and one that has been adjourned *sine die?* Will it be necessary to send out an additional notice before the meeting is held?
2. If a member who proposed a motion decides, as the discussions proceed, that he is no longer in favour of it, can he withdraw the motion and if so, what is the procedure?

   If, in fact, the motion is put to the vote and is carried and becomes a resolution, can anything subsequently be added to it?

3. You have just read out the minutes of the social committee meeting (of which you are secretary) held last month and the chairman now asks the meeting 'Is it your wish that I sign these minutes as an accurate record of the last meeting?'

One of the members objects to this and states that a particular minute is inaccurate. How will this matter be put right and how will such a procedure affect you?

Suggested solution to problem 1

A meeting that has been postponed, has in fact not taken place, although a notice will originally have been sent out calling the meeting. It may have been postponed because of sickness or inability of certain members to be present or it may have been postponed because, when the meeting was due to begin, it was found that there were insufficient members present to constitute a quorum.

On the other hand, a meeting that has been adjourned *sine die*, has taken place but will have been adjourned indefinitely, possibly to obtain more information on a point at issue or because the time constraints on the meeting had expired.

In both instances, however, the meeting will have to be called again, with the required length of notice as stipulated in the articles of association, in order to constitute a valid meeting.

Suggested solution to problem 2

If the proposer of a motion were to find himself in this situation, he may propose a motion of withdrawal which, if seconded and carried, would invalidate the first motion and all discussion would cease. It would be up to the secretary, upon instruction from the chair, to ensure that this action was recorded in the minutes as a resolution of withdrawal.

If, however, the motion of withdrawal received no support, discussion would continue and voting would take place on the original motion as normal.

With regard to the second half of the question — 'Yes', an addition may be made to the resolution. This must be proposed, seconded, and voted upon and, if carried, is termed a 'rider'; it cannot contradict or invalidate in any way —only add or clarify a point.

Suggested solution to problem 3

First of all, there is no doubt that this is a rather unusual occurrence but nevertheless if you are to take on the responsibility of secretary you must be aware of how to handle such matters.

The objecting member must firstly be asked exactly why he claims inaccuracy and then justify his claim. Once he has clarified this point, the other members of the committee will then be asked to approve the suggested correction in the minutes. If this approval is given, the chairman must alter the minutes there and then, after which he can again put the question to the meeting for the minutes to be approved and then signed.

Case study

You are Veronica Smythe, secretary/PA to the managing director of Wilfords, a chain of retail outlets selling a wide variety of household, garden, and leisure equipment.

Your buying committee meets on the third Thursday in each month at 1430 hours in the company's head office committee room at Weybridge House, Worcester. The next meeting is due to take place in December.

The Committee members are:

Mr William Greenstone (chairman) managing director
Miss Veronica Smythe (secretary)
Mr Philip Stephens (chief accountant)
Mr George Bayley (Oxford)
Miss Jean Connolly (Bournemouth)
Mr Alan Davies (West London)
Mr Jack Evison (Worcester)
Mrs Diana Forbes (Eastbourne)
Mr Tony Harwood (Exeter)
Mr James King (Norwich)
Mr Ken Patterson (Torquay)
Mrs Judith Simpson (York)
Mr Bill Smethurst (Leeds)
Miss Betty Weir (Chester)
Mr John Yates (Southampton)

You have today received a telex (Fig. 5.1) from your boss who is on a buying tour of Scandinavia investigating the possibility of the stores stocking some of the latest wood burning stoves and other items.

In the morning mail you have received details of a one-week Distribution Industries Training Board residential course for junior management that looks extremely interesting. This matter had arisen under any other business at the previous meeting and you had been requested to obtain this information.

In addition to the notes shown in Fig. 5.2 (page 59), you have also accumulated some notes for the meeting as shown in Fig. 5.3 (page 60).

```
54243  WILF  H
98674  TØJU  B     2/12/--
```

ATTENTION MISS SMYTHE
SCHEDULE DELAYED SEVERAL DAYS DUE AIRPORT WORKERS' STRIKE. EXPEDITE
DOCUMENTS FOR BUYING COMMITTEE MEETING IN A FORTNIGHT. ADDITIONAL
NOTES IN TICKLER. PREPARE MY AGENDA. ITEM FOR AGENDA — ANNUAL PRO-
DUCTS BUDGET PER BRANCH AGREED LAST BOARD MEETING AT FIVE HUNDRED
THOUSAND POUNDS. BREAKDOWN TO BE DISCUSSED — SUBMISSIONS AT
MEETING.   GREENSTONE.

```
98674  TØJU  B
54243  WILF  H
```

Figure 5.1   Telex you have received

Tasks

1. Produce the notice and agenda to be sent to the members.
2. Produce the chairman's agenda, which will be used by your boss at the meeting.
3. List details of any other documents that you should circulate with the agenda or have ready for distribution at the meeting.
4. List the jobs you would have to do apart from the routine jobs of arranging the meeting.

Suggested approach

Standard information

When you have read through the case study very carefully, you will see that there is sufficient information to compose the notice for the meeting.

As far as the ordinary agenda is concerned, you should firstly be able to list those standard items that appear on all such documents: the first three items and the last two.

Analysis of information

Now consider appropriate agenda headings by analysing the information contained in Mr Greenstone's and your own notes, the telex message, and pertinent items appearing in the mail.

Which of these items fall within the category of standard agenda headings? These details will, therefore, not appear on the ordinary agenda as separate items but don't forget them when you come to do the chairman's agenda.

Dec. Buying b'ttee – notes
Retirement of George Bayley – Formal dinner &
presentation 2 mths' time. b'ttee to approve
venue & gift. Not coming to mtg – apols.
Menus & available dates obtained from
            Regent Hotel Oxford – most likely
            Bel Air – London
            Highcliffe – B'mouth

Easter event – selection of items
① Write Hortico Ltd – give deadline for del'y
of one motor mower for mtg day. Suggest 1st
order may be 60 – 5 per store if managers
agree. Ask Veronica to arrange for mower to be
in mtg room.

Wallpaper
Suggest stop stocking. V. slow moving. Proposed
John Yates. Tony Harwood also in favour. Space
can be better used. Suggestions already requested
from branches. Chase any replies not rec'd. V.
to analyse and prepare tabulated statement
of suggestions. Copies for all.

Figure 5.2   Notes that you have accumulated for the meeting

Ordering the items
Remember that when you have a very full agenda and a meeting that has only
a limited amount of time, the most urgent matters must take precedence.

Try to put your items in order before you look at the suggested agenda (Fig.
5.4, page 60) which also includes the rationale. Once you are satisfied that you
have got your agenda into a reasonable order, you can tackle the chairman's
agenda.

Chairman's agenda
You will remember that this document is intended to assist the chairman in
guiding the meeting and must therefore contain more information than the

Selection of items – Easter event   Camp Gear Barbecues willing to supply with our logo — dyeline drawing attached (N.B. photocopies for mtg). C'tee to discuss requesting own brand name sleeve. Small charge.

Consideration of various new products for regular stock   Mother-of-pearl lampshades from Indonesia — proposed by Jean Connolly. Obtaining samples for mtg. (Phone to check if rec'd.) Stepstools from John Bailey Ltd — check samples received in stores. Also check swatches received of various finishes available — if not phone.

Drill stands - sample now in stores — send memo to arrange for drill stand to be in room well before the meeting. Man from maintenance to demonstrate? Elec. point?

Forecast of requirements of bathroom fittings   Sales targets and actual to be provided by managers as in last mins already circulated.

Cashflow   Relocation of sticking lines. Mr G. concerned money tied up in out-of-season lines: 100 leisure hammocks in Leeds. Send to coastal branches? Patterson and Connolly not keen.

Figure 5.3   Your agenda notes

The monthly meeting of the buying committee is to be held on Thursday 17 December 19-- at 1430 hours at Weybridge House.

Agenda

1. Apologies for absence.
2. Minutes of the meeting held on 19/11 — already circulated.
3. Matters arising from the minutes.
4   Retirement of Oxford manager.
5. Selection of items — Easter event.
6. Products budget.
7. Consideration of new products.
8. Discontinuation of stocking wallpaper.
9. Cashflow Problem — sticking lines.
10. Date of next meeting.
11. Any other business.

Veronica Smythe
Secretary

7 December 19--

Figure 5.4   Task 1. Suggested agenda and agenda rationale

Agenda rationale

1-3.	Must appear in that order.
4.	- Decisions will be reached rapidly.
	- Retirement very near — cannot be left.
5.	Easter is not too far away and preparations need to be made and delivery dates considered.
6.	Managers need to establish how the money is going to be divided in various sections before they can consider new products.
7.	Follows logically from **6**.
8,9.	Regarding items about to be changed or discontinued — could be settled out of committee.
10.	While this item often appears in textbooks as the last item, in practical terms it is the final item where a definite decision by the meeting is required.
11.	No definite decisions should be made on items brought up under AOB. Members may therefore feel free to leave the meeting, if necessary.

Figure 5.4   Task 1. (*continued*)

brief headings on the ordinary agenda. On the other hand, it should not be so full as to be confusing.

As you work through the items on your ordinary agenda, check the information you have and extract the details that appertain to that particular agenda heading. These should then appear as fuller items in your chairman's agenda.

Don't forget that you have omitted points in the ordinary agenda that must now appear on the chairman's agenda.

By now you should be in a position to draft out your chairman's agenda. If you're in any doubt at this point you can check the suggested chairman's agenda (Fig. 5.5, page 62).

The other details

This is perhaps one of the most important aspects of this study. In the real situation you should not wander into a meeting ill-prepared, with the members only half-informed.

Again, working item by item, check and make sure that you know what you would have to do and prepare, in readiness for the meeting. You could note these jobs on the draft agenda so that you have a ready-made checklist.

You can then decide which documents need preparation and which tasks need to be done (Fig. 5.6, page 62 and Fig. 5.7, page 63):

- Before the agenda is circulated.
- Prior to the meeting.
- For presentation at the meeting.

1. Apologies for absence: George Bayley.   1.
2. Minutes of previous meeting.   2.
3. Matters arising: 3.
   - DITB residential course for junior managers.
     Details prepared.
   - Forecast bathroom fittings — sales targets and
     actual.
4. Retirement of George Bayley: 4.
   - Menus and hotel letters attached: Regent Hotel,
     Oxford; Bel Air, London; Highcliffe,
     Bournemouth.
5. Selection of items for Easter Event: 5.
   - Motor mower — sample, 5 per store.
   - Camp Gear Barbecues — logo — photocopy.
     Discuss own brand name sleeve.
6. Products budget: 6.
   - Breakdown requested — see memo attached.
7. Consideration of new products: 7.
   - Stepstools — sample — colour swatches.
   - Drill stands — sample and demo.
   - Mother-of-pearl lampshades sample — Jean
     Connolly.
8. Discontinuation stocking wallpaper: 8.
   - To be proposed John Yates.
   - To be seconded Tony Harwood.
   - Tabulated list other suggestions.
9. Cashflow problems: 9.
   - Bill Smethurst has not moved 100 leisure ham-
     mocks. Restricting his buying. Move to coastal
     branches? Bournemouth? Torquay? Objections
     may be raised.
10. Any other business: 10.
   - Brief comments on trip to Scandinavia.
11. Date of next meeting 16/1.   11.

Figure 5.5 Task 2. Chairman's agenda

- Spare copies of minutes of last meeting.
- Spare copies of agenda.
- 15 photocopies of information regarding DITB course.
- 15 photocopies of Camp Gear Logo.
- 15 photocopies of bathroom fittings — sales figures (target and actual).
- 15 photocopies of suggestions for alternative lines to wallpaper.

The last two prepared after 12/12.
Collate leaflets of hotels and menus re. George Bayley presentation.

Figure 5.6 Task 3. Documents for circulation at the meeting

- Circulate with notice and agenda: memo to branch managers. Board agrees budget figure of £500 000 per store. Your suggested breakdown will be discussed at the meeting. Request alternative lines to be carried if wallpaper discontinued. Required by 12 December.
- Letter to Hortico — motor mower to be delivered by 12 December. Suggest initial order of 60 may be required.
- Phone Jean Connolly — samples of pearl lampshades obtained?
- Phone stores — check samples received of stepstools and swatches. If not — telex John Bailey giving deadline date of 12 December.

  Memo to stores after 12 December

- Date of buying committee meeting — request samples of motor mower, stepstool, and drill stand to be in the committee room Weybridge House by 1230 hours. (Copy to maintenance with note.)

Figure 5.7 Task 4. Jobs that need to be done

One step further

This case study has provided you with a great deal of information that has enabled you to prepare for the meeting of the buying committee. In order to take the case study to its logical conclusion, you must be able to produce the minutes of that meeting.

Let us assume that you were unable to attend the meeting and notes were compiled in your absence by the chairman on the chairman's agenda. From these, draft out the minutes of the buying committee meeting ensuring that you have an action column in your layout (Fig. 5.8, page 64).

Case study

You are Linda Peters, committee secretary to the welfare committee, which meets every month. The meetings frequently over-run the allotted time resulting in frustration and dissatisfaction and so members are lapsing in attendance. The committee chairman, who is also the company secretary, is involved in a number of other committees and has asked you to make suggestions as to how the meetings could be run more efficiently.

Suggested approach

The first point to be realized in this problem is that meetings involve people and no human is infallible. Ask yourself, therefore, who could be to blame?

- Is it the chairman?
- Is it yourself?
- Is it the other members?

Chairman's agenda

1. Apologies for absence:
    George Bayley.

2. Minutes of previous meeting.

3. Matters arising:
    DITB residential course for junior managers.
    Details prepared.
    Forecast bathroom fittings - sales targets
    and actual.

4. Retirement of George Bayley:
    Menus and Hotel letters attached:
    Regent Hotel, Oxford; Bel Air, London;
    Highcliffe, Bournemouth.

5. Selection of items for Easter
    event:
    Motor mower - sample.   5 per store.
    Camp Gear Barbecues - logo - photocopy.
    Discuss own brand name sleeve.

6. Products budget:
    Breakdown requested - see memo attached.

7. Consideration of new products:
    Stepstools - sample - colour swatches.
    Drill stands - sample and demo.
    Mother-of-pearl lampshades sample - Jean
    Connolly.

8. Discontinuation stocking wallpaper:
    To be proposed John Yates.
    To be seconded Tony Harwood.
    Tabulated list other suggestions.

9. Cash flow problems:
    Bill Smethurst has not moved 100 leisure
    hammocks.   Restricting his buying.   Move
    to coastal branches?   Bournemouth?   Torquay?
    Objections may be raised.

10. Any other business:
    Brief comments on trip to Scandinavia.

11. Date of next meeting 16/1.

1. G.B. ✓

2. ✓

3. Suggested that two from Soton,
    York & Torquay go. names to be put
    fwd for next course.
    Gold-plated taps slow - suggest
    discontinue line - prop. BW, sec.
    JS: "It was agreed that when
    existing stocks were exhausted
    the line of gold-plated taps
    would be discontinued." Onyx-
    finish range sales up - all stores
    to stock.

4. Some discussion. Regent finally
    OK. 2nd Friday Feb. WG to put
    to next Bod Mtg suggestions for
    GB presentation: carriage clock,
    cine camera, video recorder.

5. mower not available - no
    discussion. Ensure del'y for
    next mtg. Action VS.
    Prop AD   Sec JK. Agreed that
    CG Barbecues supply without
    a logo but with co sleeve.

6. Breakdown submitted for
    presentation to board. PS
    to produce amalgamated
    statement. Managers to retain
    autonomy.

7. Stepstools to Chester, Exeter,
    Worcester, Eastbourne & W London
    in avocado and black washable.
    Report progress next mtg.
    After demo mtg felt current stand
    stocked more satis. Action VS-
    stores to return sample.
    JC produced samples and acclaimed
    high quality. Trial order of 50
    to be distributed throughout stores.

8. Resolved: that group would
    discontinue stocking wallpaper
    once current stocks exhausted.
    Of suggestions kitchen displays
    most favourably rec'd - JE to cost
    and investigate space needed.

9. Vehemently opposed by JC
    and KP. JY willing to take
    40. Rest BS to advertise
    locally at cost.

10. WG reported on visit to Scand.
    Impressed with stoves seen.
    Literature to be circulated to
    branches Action VS Samples
    being sent for next mtg.

11. ✓

Figure 5.8   Anotated version of chairman's agenda

Let's look at it first of all from the chairman's angle. He's a very busy man — so where might he be at fault?

1. Is he arriving late at the meeting?
2. Is he ill-prepared for the meeting?
3. Does he not control the meeting efficiently?

Now take a look at yourself.

4. Are your preparations for the venue adequate?
5. Do you help the chairman through the meeting?
6. Do you ensure that documents and information are prepared and distributed beforehand?
7. Are you working in close liaison with the chairman?
8. Are you working in close liaison with the committee members?

Now that you have analysed where the chairman and you may be at fault, consider where the other members of the committee may be creating problems:

9. Are they informing you of their intentions to attend?
10. Are they studying information and preparing for the meeting?
11. Are they punctual?

In the real situation many of these questions would be rejected as invalid. Indeed they would have to be rejected otherwise the situation in the meeting would not only be difficult but absolutely chaotic!

However, for the purposes of this problem, try to evolve a possible area of improvement in answer to each question. This will ensure that you think logically and thoroughly about the possible causes of the meetings running over their allotted time.

Our suggested answer is approached in exactly the same way and appears in Fig. 5.9.

Question
number

1. ● Closer liaison with the chairman's secretary would prevent over-booking his diary and also ensure a reminder is given to him about the meeting.
2. ● Check with the chairman's secretary that the documents have been received. This provides an opportunity to ask that she makes sure that he has time to consider them before the meeting.
3. ● If too much time is spent by members in discussing the various agenda points a warning light could be used to limit the time spent on each item.
   ● There are many ways in which the secretary can help the chairman to control the meeting and these are dealt with under the appropriate question number.

Figure 5.9 Suggested answer to welfare committee case study (*continued on page 66*)

4.
- Always prepare the room and ensure that nothing is overlooked that could cause delays. Arrange for refreshments to be served at an appropriate time and for a limited period.
- Be in the room 15 minutes before the start of the meeting to ensure that early arrivals are not waiting around and so can avoid the last minute rush to the seats.
- Ensure that the meeting room has not been booked too closely beforehand and, hence, that there is no danger of the previous meeting impinging on your time.
- Ensure that you take into the meeting room the attendance register, reference books, spare minutes and agendas, and extra notepaper.
- Inform the receptionist of the venue of the meeting and organize direction signs to try to ensure that everyone arrives on time, particularly newcomers.
- Use the warning light outside the meeting room to ensure that there are no interruptions.
- Another measure to make sure there are no interruptions is to inform the switchboard and give them a number to which calls should be redirected.

5.
- Prepare the chairman's agenda with plenty of useful notes to enable him to be in control of the meeting.
- Sort out the various papers required during the meeting into the appropriate order.
- Use flagging devices on relevant files and documents to speed up access to information.

6.
- Provide the chairman with notes on any new members of the committee to enable him to prepare a welcome.
- Ensure that the chairman has his agenda and accompanying papers well in advance of the meeting to enable him to study them.
- Prepare and distribute the minutes and any other documents before the meeting for prior perusal.

7.
- When preparing the agenda try to ensure that the most important topics are discussed first so that less important matters can be left over if necessary.
- You should be aware of any particularly controversial items to be discussed and warn the chairman accordingly.
- Other points that require close liaison with the chairman are given under their appropriate question heading.

8.
- When preparing agenda items, check that any action to be taken from the last meeting has, in fact, been taken and that well-prepared reports will be presented to the meeting.
- Your relationship with the various members of the committee should be good enough to ensure that any controversial items likely to be raised at the meeting that come through on the office grapevine are passed over to you.

9.
- Members should automatically pass to the secretary their apologies if they are unable to attend but the secretary may have to double check in order to ensure that a quorum will be present. This prevents the delay in starting a meeting when one is wondering whether a member is going to turn up or not.

Figure 5.9 Suggested answer to welfare committee case study (*continued on page 67*)

10.● One cannot force members to give full consideration to information that is circulated to them but the chairman must insist on members coming to the meeting well-prepared if the information has already been distributed to them.

11.● Again this is a situation that is difficult to control but it is up to the chairman to press on with the meeting whether members are present or not (once a quorum has been mustered, of course).

Figure 5.9 Suggested answer to welfare committee case study (*continued*)

One step further

As a result of your helpful suggestions and the consequent smooth running of the welfare committee, the company secretary has now asked for your help in the preparations for the company's annual general meeting.

How will these preparations differ from those you undertake for the welfare committee?

Planning a safe journey

He regretted that he was not a bird, and could not be in two places at once.

SIR BOYLE ROCHE (1743-1807)

There are very few secretarial jobs that do not involve making travel arrangements of one kind or another whether for home or overseas travel. For the inexperienced secretary it is easy to make a fool of oneself or cause inconvenience to your employer without a little forethought. You do not, for example, ask your boss if he wants you to reserve a sleeper on the train if it turns out to be only a two-hour journey; nor do you arrange a dinner appointment when he has just landed in New York after a transatlantic flight!

Even though you will by now have studied the principles of making travel arrangements, there are still many points to be borne in mind that tend not to be found in secretarial textbooks.

Your careful planning and attention to detail will make all the difference to your boss travelling in safety and comfort and arriving at the first meeting fresh and relaxed.

Do you know?
1. How to read all kinds of maps easily? Your ability should include road maps, ordnance survey maps, town plans (especially when a one-way system exists), and atlases.
2. How to find your way round a timetable whether it be for trains, planes, or ferries? You should be aware of the different formats timetables can have and always check first on the key symbols used. It is also well to remember that arrivals are always given in local time.
3. What the main world currencies are and where to find out the current rates of exchange? What is the present legal position with regard to the transfer of monies in and out of the country?
4. What paperwork is involved? Where are documents such as passports, visas, insurance certificates, tickets, and vaccination certificates obtained? When do they need to be obtained?
5. The difference between an itinerary and an appointment card?
6. What the main reference books are for making travel arrangements? Are you familiar with such reference sources as AA/RAC publications, good food guides, European travel guides, and the world airways and shipping guides?
7. There are also many service organizations who can greatly assist when making

travel arrangements: travel, hotel, and tourist information centres, chambers of commerce and trade, embassies, and consulates.

Snippets
1. If your boss has to cross the international dateline he may lose or gain a day depending on whether he is travelling from east to west or west to east respectively.
2. Maintain contact with your local chamber of trade and commerce to keep up to date on current market trends. This is especially useful if your company is involved in the export market. They organize trade missions to developing export areas and can set up contacts for your company.
3. The booklets entitled *Hints to Exporters* covering specific geographical areas provide vital information for the new traveller to that area. They are produced by the Department of Trade and Industry and are obtainable from the British and Overseas Trade Board.
4. The *Travel Trade Directory* is published annually and lists all travel agents in the UK and gives useful information about all forms of travel.
5. *World Calendar of Holidays* published by Morgan Guaranty Trust lists public holidays throughout the world, and time differences.
6. Travicom — 160 travel agents in the UK have direct VDU access to 21 major airlines, providing up-to-the-minute booking schedules, flight connections, special passenger requirements, and instant confirmation of bookings.
7. If you or your employer use credit cards, it is possible to insure against their loss by paying a modest annual sum. An immediate telephone call to the insurer, after the loss, will protect you.

Short problems
1. It is planned that some of the export sales representatives in your company will be travelling to the EEC countries to develop new outlets for your products.

   What precautions would have to be taken to ensure that, if anyone had an accident or was taken ill, the financial consequences would not be too heavy for your company?
2. Your boss is visiting a country in which there is a high risk of pick-pocketing and stealing in public places.

   How will you ensure that he will not be without funds?

Suggested solution to problem 1
1. Reciprocal arrangements for health insurance purposes exist between all EEC countries. In order to guarantee such cover when visiting one of these countries the procedure is as follows:
   - DHSS SA30 gives information about medical benefits available to temporary visitors to EEC countries.
   - DHSS CM1 — this form must be completed in order to obtain the

necessary certificate of entitlement to medical benefits (Form E111).

- Form E111 certifies that the person covered and dependants are entitled to medical benefits under the EEC Social Security Regulations for a period covering stay abroad. The visitor must obtain reimbursement of any sums due before leaving the country concerned. Receipts must be obtained for medical treatment and for prescriptions. Persons are only entitled to medical treatment for which an urgent need arises.
- DHSS SA36 — *How to Get Medical Treatment in the Other EEC Countries* — is an advisory leaflet that should accompany the traveller.

2. Taking out a private 'all-risks' insurance policy would cover all other eventualities including long-stay hospitalization.

3. Regular medical examinations should form part of the contract of employment for such employees, thus ensuring that they are not exempt from insurance cover, and are always aware of any health risks.

Suggested solution to problem 2

1. No matter how high the risk, a small amount of cash is essential to cover the incidental expenses needed on arrival. For convenience some foreign currency should be obtained before leaving this country.

2. In order to safeguard this cash your employer may consider wearing a money belt.

3. One of the safest ways of having money available when abroad is in the form of travellers' cheques. For added security, however, you — as well as your boss — should have a list of the numbers of the cheques in case of loss or theft. Once the issuing bank has been informed of the disappearance of the cheques, the liability for accepting a fraudulent signature on the subsequent cashing of cheques rests with the bank or bureau de change that cashes the cheques.

4. Taking a selection of credit cards will ensure that goods and services can be paid for at any time and in any part of the world: e.g., Barclaycard Visa, American Express, Access, Diner's Club.

5. It is often not appreciated that local currency can be obtained, and sometimes goods and services paid for, by using an ordinary joint stock bank cheque book and the special overseas Eurocheque card. It is advisable to look out for the Eurocheque sign.

6. An international money transfer can be arranged from this country provided the full name and address of the beneficiary is known together with the name and address of the paying bank overseas. Sterling or currency can be transferred. If monies are transferred in this way by cable, a fee is payable.

7. A draft may also be sent abroad if the name of the payee can be provided, together with the country and current town of residence. The bank will then send the money to an appropriate bank near to the place of residence of the payee. No account is necessary and the monies will be paid out upon proof of identity.

8. Most large hotels offer the use of their safe and a refusal to use this service would render the client liable if items over a certain value were stolen from the room.

9. A final safeguard would be to take out an 'all risks' insurance policy to give protection against loss of funds.

Case study

You are secretary to Mr Ian Nash, European sales manager of Young Fashions Ltd, a fashion manufacturing and marketing company that sells in Europe and is based in Bath, Avon.

He is preparing to visit a number of fashion buyers in Paris, Brussels, and Amsterdam during May. It is Monday and when you arrived in the office this morning you found a tape, the transcription of which can be seen in Fig. 6.1.

Details of the appointments already confirmed appear in Fig. 6.2.

Tasks

1. Write to Monsieur Tilleul confirming the appointment for 18 May at 11.30 in his office.
2. Prepare an itinerary to cover the trip, including Mr and Mrs Nash's weekend in Amsterdam and their return.
3. Obtain information on places of interest in Amsterdam.
4. Apart from the itinerary, list the jobs you would have to do to ensure that Mr Nash was well-prepared for his trip.

Suggested approach

At first glance, this problem may appear to be a little daunting but with logical thinking and a planned approach a reasonable itinerary can be arrived at without too much difficulty.

First of all, check that you have all the materials you will need. It is vital that you pencil in all arrangements as you decide on them so that you can take an overall view of the situation before making any firm arrangements.

1. *Getting him to Paris*

   The first thing you have to do is decide on the starting out time and this is most easily arrived at by working back from the first appointment.

23 April

As I shan't be in the office for the rest of the week could you begin arrangements for my forthcoming trip to Europe bearing the following in mind, and liaise with our usual travel agents for the tickets?

1. I've decided to go by car in view of all the samples I shall have to take. Needless to say I'll use the motorways whenever possible. Please check on tolls for me.
2. I'll hover from Dover to Calais — it's motorway into Paris that way.
3. Neither my wife nor I have had the opportunity to stay in Amsterdam so we've decided to spend the weekend there and would like to stay in a small but comfortable hotel. She'll be in Manchester all that week so will fly from there — please arrange it with the agency for her to arrive as near to 1800 as possible so that I will be free to meet her. We'll take a couple of days' holiday and return from the Hook of Holland on the Monday ferry. Can you get some information on what to see in Amsterdam? We both like art as you know.
4. Jean Tilleul rang me at home last night and I've arranged to see him in his office on 18 May at about 1130 and we'll go out to lunch. He's going to arrange for me to meet a couple of prospective customers that afternoon. Perhaps you would confirm this in writing with Jean. His address is Monsieur Jean Tilleul, Fashion Critic, Publications Marie-Claire, 127 Bd Charlemagne, Bruxelles.
5. I'd like to take the following with me:
   - Swatches of autumn skirt materials in full colour range together with sketches of designs. George Dickinson of York promised them by the end of this week. If there are any problems I'll call on my way back from Scotland later this week.
   - I've arranged for the knitted suit in three designs planned for the autumn to be made up here. Make sure they're packed properly. I'll also need sample charts of available colours.
   - Will our brochure be ready? Mike Oldfield took shots of the blouses and knitwear last week. Print room doing a mock-up for Tuesday. Get it to me in Edinburgh on Wednesday. Janine Hetherington, the freelance, is doing the translation into French. Should be ready today (Monday). I'll take a selection in both English and French.
   - James Anderson is working on UK prices. Can you produce a tabular statement in pounds, francs (French and Belgian) and guilders?

Figure 6.1   Transcript of tape left by Mr Ian Nash

The first appointment is at 0900 in Paris and it would therefore seem reasonable that Mr Nash should arrive the night before. If you aim for a 2000 arrival in Paris, first decide how long, both in terms of distance and time, Paris is from Calais. Consult a map or distance chart to find out the mileage and this can then be converted into time in the following manner: as the journey would be covered mainly by motorway, an average of 100 k.p.h. (62 m.p.h.) is quite reasonable with an extra half an hour added on for every three hours of journey to allow for short stops. This calculation should now give you the time it will take Mr Nash to drive from Calais to Paris.

May	May
Monday 15	Thursday 18
Tuesday *Paris* 16 0900 Claude Dupont - Buyer Jeune Textiles SA 111-5 Bd Raspail 1300 Lunch with Giles Mass Tricotique Av Victor Hugo 1600 Yvette Filet - buyer Mode Boutiques SA 291 Quai d'Orsay	Friday *Amsterdam* 19 1400 M. van Eyck – designer Meet Amsterdam Hilton (Has sent samples of his work – IN to take)
Wednesday 17 1100 Jacques Maartens Sérénade SA Place de la République Rheims 1930 Fédération Belge des for Industries de Vêtement 2000 et Confection Restaurant Ravenstein Rue Ravenstein Brussels	Saturday 20 Sunday 21

Figure 6.2 Appointments already confirmed for Mr Nash

2. *Getting him to Calais*

Once you know at what time Mr Nash needs to leave the French port in order to arrive in Paris at 2000, you can than begin to think about a suitable hovercraft flight. There are, however, several points to be considered before you consult the timetable:

(a) Allow time for Mr Nash to disembark and clear customs (approximately one hour).

(b) Do you need to add on any extra time for Mr Nash to have a meal *en route*?

(c) At this time of year France is one hour ahead of England and therefore the apparent hovercraft crossing time is one hour forty minutes.

Now consult the hovercraft timetable in your possession and decide on a suitable flight.

3. *Getting him to Dover*

Once you have decided on a flight you can now consider travel in England and work out when Mr Nash should leave Bath. Look at a route map and decide on the most appropriate route. Convert into time-terms using 62 m.p.h. average for motorway driving and 30 m.p.h. average for normal roads unless there is obviously a large stretch of dual carriageway when you can increase the average to 40 m.p.h.

You have now achieved what is perhaps the most difficult part of the itinerary — getting him to his first destination safely and in plenty of time.

4. *Settling him in Paris*

You can now turn your attention to the rest of the itinerary and start by considering a hotel in Paris bearing the following thoughts in mind:

(a) Mr Nash has a car and will therefore need a garage.

(b) Identify where the appointments are in Paris.

(c) Is there a hotel in that particular area?

(d) What facilities will he require in the hotel?

Once you have decided on the hotel, book a room for the necessary time. As Paris is an exceptionally busy city, particularly in the spring and early summer, there is the possibility that the hotel you have chosen may be fully booked for the nights you want. You should, therefore, telephone or send a telex to save time and you will be able to make an alternative booking if your first choice of hotel cannot help you.

5. *Getting him to Brussels*

Mr Nash has an appointment in Rheims which is north-east of Paris. You must work out, therefore, the length of journey from Paris to Rheims and from Rheims to Brussels. Using the formula given, calculate distance and convert to time.

6. *Settling him in Brussels*

Establish the location of Mr Nash's appointments and decide on a suitable hotel in Brussels. He will stay there for two nights so that on 18 May he has a complete day free from driving.

7. *Getting him to Amsterdam*

On 19 May Mr Nash has an appointment at 1400 and so will be able to make quite a leisurely start from Brussels. Make your calculations in terms of distance and time for the journey from Brussels to Amsterdam. Allow extra time as both Brussels and Amsterdam are very busy and highly congested cities and can take some time to get in and out of.

8. *Settling him in Amsterdam*

Once you have found a suitable hotel, phone them and book a double room for the nights of Friday, Saturday, and Sunday. Mr Nash should have time to check in the hotel before his appointment with Mr van Eyck.

9. *Getting Mrs Nash to Amsterdam*

Identify a suitable flight for Mrs Nash and ask the travel agent to make the booking when you reserve the other tickets. Special invoicing arrangements will probably have to be made for this ticket, as it is not a company expense.

10. *The return journey*

Mr and Mrs Nash will return on the Hook of Holland ferry to Harwich. They will drive to the ferry port from Amsterdam. Calculate the time it will take them bearing in mind you will not have the same flexibility with regard to time as ferries operate far less frequently.

11. *The bits and pieces*

Tolls and motorways   The AA and RAC European handbooks will tell you whether tolls are payable or not. Make sure this information is shown on the itinerary.

Places of interest in Amsterdam   Your local travel agent should be able to give you this information or you could contact the Dutch National Tourist Office in London.

Money supply   While you are not specifically asked to do this in the list of tasks, you should order appropriate quantities of the right currencies from the bank together with any traveller's cheques.

Insurance   Both for Mr Nash and the car. As he is visiting EEC countries he should be in possession of a form E111. He may also wish to take out additional personal insurance and this can be included in the five-star insurance schemes available from motoring organizations, which also includes breakdown cover and green card insurance for the car. (Extra insurance cover is not essential but the reciprocal arrangements that exist only apply up to the minimum legal requirement for the country being visited.)

Passport   Ensure that Mr Nash's passport is still current. Even though officially it is not needed when visiting EEC countries, as we in Britain do not have any other form of identification, a passport must be carried.

Samples   Check with Mr George Dickinson of York that swatches will be ready by the end of the week. Contact Mr Nash if there is any problem. Arrange for Mr Dickinson to contact you when the swatches have been dispatched. Follow up every two days until they are received.

- Check with the design and machine room to ensure that the suits will be ready and ask for advice with reference to packing and care. Ensure that

colour charts will be prepared and well-presented.
- Check with Mike Oldfield that Mr Nash decided which shots he wanted and then with the print room to verify that the mock-up will be ready the next day. Transmit by facsimile a copy of the brochure to Mr Nash in Edinburgh for his approval.
- Check with Janine Hetherington that the translation is complete. Ensure it is in the office by the next day and send it to the print room for reproduction.

Prices Obtain prices from James Anderson, check with the bank and then accounts on the exchange rate to be used, convert the prices, and produce a tabular statement.

Documentation Gather together those files, documents, road maps, and street maps Mr Nash is likely to need.

One step further
Indicate the organizational problems that might arise during his absence. Suggest how these might be anticipated and/or obviated.

Long problem
Your employer, Paul Davidson, is the managing director of a company that makes and sells scientific instruments in Maidenhead. He has just called you into his office and this is the conversation that ensued:

PD 'What did you think of this invitation to go to the spring Guangzhou Export Commodities Fair? I presume it has come as a result of a meeting I had with Chinese delegates at the trade fair I attended in Tokyo last year.'

U 'Yes. I seem to remember filing a card from a Chinese organization.'

PD 'Now, what *was* their name? Oh yes — the China National Instruments Import and Export Corporation. I think I'm right but perhaps you would like to check that? Anyhow they were very interested in some of the products on our stand and, although the purpose of this fair is to sell Chinese products, I believe some invaluable contacts could be made. I think it would be well worth the effort to make the trip to this fair because, who knows, from the contacts we make it might be possible to have a stand at one of the exhibitions that I believe are held from time to time in the major large cities in China.'

U 'Do you think there is much potential for our products in China?'

PD 'Well China is certainly a rapidly developing country and as we have seen with Latin America, the sales of our products have soared.'

U 'So, really we can't afford to turn down this invitation as our products obviously made a good impression.'

PD 'Yes that's true. I think once you're in there, they seem to like to remain with the same companies.'

U 'Just a second — isn't it in April when you are planning to go to the fair in Tel Aviv where we have a stand?'

PD 'Yes it is but I could spend about a week in Guangzhou and then go on from there to Israel.'

U 'Where is Guangzhou? I must admit I've never heard of it.'

PD 'I think you will find that originally it was called Canton but I believe it had another name too. At any rate, I think it is relatively near to Hong Kong. I know that the fair isn't for another three months but as I anticipate being extremely busy for a few weeks, I'd like you to make some investigations for me. Heaven knows how long it will take for a visa to come through and we really must be well organized for this trip!'

U 'I don't know very much at all about China so I shall look forward to tackling this. Thank goodness we have a good commercial section in our public library!'

PD 'Give some thought to what needs to be done and we'll have another chat about it tomorrow. Pop down to the library and see if you can get a few pointers. Perhaps while you are there you can see if you can get any up-to-date statistics on import trends in China, particularly with relation to our sort of products.'

U 'Fine. I'll see what I can do.'

Suggested approach

Your boss has given you some good starting points to this problem by suggesting that there are separate areas that will require your investigation in order to prepare him for this trip. Jot down some of the more obvious ones that come immediately to mind before reading on. (You will need a diary in order to give this problem more realism.)

The journey

Investigate direct flights from Heathrow to Guangzhou. Look at a map to decide on the next possibility if Guangzhou is impossible. Once you have found what seems to be a suitable route, consider the frequency of the flights and the connection times.

What are the travel possibilities from the point of arrival to Guangzhou?

As there is a second stage to this journey, it would be advisable to sort out all the travel arrangements first, so that arrival and departure dates are known. You should therefore plan suitable travel arrangements from Guangzhou to Tel Aviv. The availability of flights may affect the departure point.

For the purpose of this problem let us assume that Mr Davidson will return from Tel Aviv to London with the sales team and therefore arrangements will be made separately.

Once you have investigated all of these points and planned the travel arrangements to suit Mr Davidson's schedules, close liaison with a travel agent is essential to ensure as far as possible that no hitches can arise.

Visa

As Mr Davidson travels a great deal his passport must always be current. However obtaining visas can be a lengthy process.

Is a visa required for

- The People's Republic of China? (Such documentation may not be necessary for Hong Kong.)
- Israel?

Check with the appropriate embassies on the likely processing time. Two possible problems arise here:

1. In order to obtain a visa, the passport must be surrendered for checking which, if two visas are necessary, could mean that the passport is away for a considerable length of time.
2. Mr Davidson may, in the three-month period, need to use his passport, so a check should be made to see if there is any way of short-cutting the bureaucratic process.

Health regulations

1. Check on health regulations bearing in mind any transit points.
2. Is any special medication needed? Does Mr Davidson keep the regular vaccinations up to date?
3. Are any re-vaccinations due? New ones needed? (Before making appointments consider possible side-effects that may hinder diary commitments.)

Climate and clothing

By carefully studying the climatic conditions and the variations that can occur, discomfort and illness can be prevented by giving appropriate advice on clothing and medication to be taken.

Accommodation

Booking a hotel should not be delayed as it is a very large trade fair.

Investigate the possibilities bearing your employer's personal preferences in mind, using appropriate reference books.

Money

Check on exchange control regulations that exist in the the UK and those that govern the import of funds into The People's Republic of China.

Consult the bank for advice regarding an appropriate amount of currency to obtain for both countries to be visited, the facility of changing travellers' cheques in both countries (are sterling, dollar, or currency cheques more appropriate?), and the use of credit and cheque cards.

Insurance

Look at all the possible risks this trip will involve and find a suitable policy.

You have now considered all the general areas that must be covered when planning intercontinental travel, but there are several specific ones that will affect the success of the trip from a business point of view.

How are you going to prepare your boss so that he is ready to pursue the interest in your company's products?

Have you any ideas? List these before reading on.

Samples

Assuming that a selection of the instruments are portable — what arrangements need to be made for taking them out of this country on the understanding that they would be returned and what are the regulations governing the import of such samples into The People's Republic and re-exporting if necessary?

Literature

Are there any restrictions on the way in which literature is presented and can appropriate translations be obtained?

Advertising

Investigate the possibility of taking promotional material, e.g. TV films.

Statistics

Research up-to-date figures for the import of scientific instruments.

Communications

What are the communication links between Britain and The People's Republic of China?

Make out a list of government bodies in the UK or The People's Republic that can provide information for anyone hoping to enter into the Chinese market.

Outings

As Mr Davidson is likely to be in China for at least a week, find out what there is to see and where there is to go.

One step further

As a result of Mr Davidson's visit to The People's Republic of China, many useful contacts have been made and he has arranged to receive a delegation of six representatives from the China National Instruments Import and Export Corporation, who will be coming to tour your factories and assess production capacity with a view to placing substantial orders.

Mr Davidson has asked you to make all the necessary arrangements, including an itinerary for this important trip to cover visits to your company's factories in Lincoln, Carlisle, and Carmarthen, as well as the Maidenhead head office. It is anticipated that they will spend two days at each factory and a total of nine days in the UK.

Part Three

Where to find it

Can you find it?

A man should keep his little brain attic stocked with all the furniture that he is likely to use, and the rest he can put away in the lumberroom of his library where he can get it if he wants it.

SIR ARTHUR CONAN DOYLE (1859-1930)

To many students — and even to some qualified and working secretaries — filing may be a tedious task and there could be some truth in this if we are thinking about the endless putting away of papers that have no sequence, that are difficult to identify because they appear not to fit into the system, and that have accumulated as a result of several weeks of having had 'no time to file'.

Nevertheless filing is important because papers must be kept for record and reference purposes and a well-defined system is essential to ensure quick access when information is needed. Unfortunately it is difficult to give the various filing methods validity and reality until one is actually in the working situation and that piece of paper is needed *urgently!*

Having an open mind

There is little point in entering a job that involves filing (or the supervision thereof) with preconceived ideas of what it should be like. It is preferable to have in your mind the various methods and the variety of equipment available so that a comparison can be made with the actual situation. Nor should any snap decisions be made. The filing system with which you will have to deal may well have been in existence for some considerable time and its idiosyncracies will have evolved to suit a particular set of circumstances at a particular time. But it may not now be the most satisfactory one. You must however give yourself time to evaluate the system before putting forward your own ideas. By the same token, once you have decided that the system could be improved by making certain changes do not hesitate to recommend them. *Never* introduce a new filing feature without reference to the other people involved — the ideal filing system is not the one that makes you indispensable! This only antagonizes, infuriates, and frustrates other users, and that almost certainly means your boss.

The hardware

It is normally difficult to change the hardware at your disposal unless you are entering new offices or the offices are being refurbished. Nevertheless unsuitable equipment should not deter you from adapting and making the best use of it.

Remember: an efficient filing system can be kept in an orange-box.

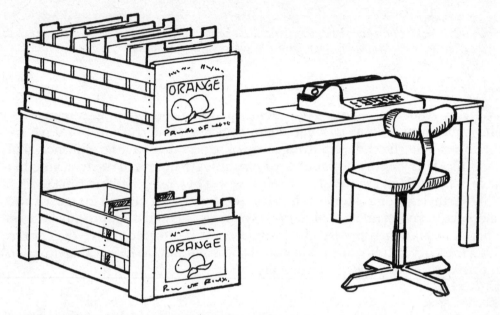

An efficient filing system can be kept in an orange box

Developing a tidy mind

In the modern office the term 'file' has many different connotations, and is no longer confined to a set of documents in a manilla or pocket folder.

You can probably accept that files are kept on microfilm as a fiche, jacket, or reel, but have you considered that files are kept in electronic form when using a computer or word processor and may be stored on magnetic tape, magnetic card, floppy disc, or rigid disc?

Unlike the metal filing cabinet, an electronic store only allows one file to be accessed to screen at a time and this must be committed back to file before another one can be extracted. It simply cannot cope with a stack of files scattered all over its CPU! This is an excellent principle that should be carried over when working at your desk with traditional files. When referring to a file you should, if possible, extract the information required and then put the folder away. A desk strewn with files and bits of paper creates confusion and disorganization. This results in mistakes being made, time being lost, and documents being mislaid.

When putting new files into electronic store they must have a name — no name, no identification, no file. This is another good principle that should be carried through to paper files. Nothing is gained from shoving a few sheets of paper into an unmarked folder and thinking 'I'll remember those are there'. In our experience, the chances are, you don't!

Even when dealing with a traditional filing system, defining and identifying papers and their contents for filing purposes does undoubtedly help the development of a tidy, logical approach to other tasks. (It can even help on the domestic front with an efficient system of filing bills and other documents and such a system can be extended to include the larder and freezer!)

The ideal
Your paper filing system should be something of which you are proud and should include:

- The logical sequencing of file names.
- The chronological sequencing of documents within the files.
- A clear pre-sorting system to minimize paper handling.
- A defined system of paper movement and replacement.

An efficiently run system creates confidence in all users to access and retrieve information rapidly and easily.

Do you know?
1. That *filing method* (software) + *filing equipment* (hardware) = filing system?
2. The difference between and the advantages and disadvantages of jackets, fiches, and aperture cards?
3. The space-saving effected by the use of microfilm?
4. The main paper filing methods and equipment used?
5. The usefulness of tickler, pending, and absent files?
6. The uses, advantages, and disadvantages of the various indexing equipment available?

Snippets
1. Directory enquiries have directories on microfilm and use readers to obtain the appropriate page.
2. Every microfilmed series of documents must have a certificate of origin and a certificate of authenticity signed by an executive of the company to assure its acceptability in law.
3. Microfilm jackets are available with a mixture of 8, 16, and 35 mm channels that enables all inter-related documents to be stored together.

4. Computer output microfilm recorders convert computer systems outputs direct to microfilm images.
5. Large companies with extensive records (e.g., insurance companies) have found automated filing and retrieval systems to be economically viable. Requests are keyed in from ouside the file store and files are selected and moved by means of a miniature crane and placed on a document conveyor via which they are automatically routed by computer control to the relevant person. Installations are usually at basement level. The advantages of such systems are speed of retrieval and high density of storage. Disadvantages are cost and risk of breakdown.
6. Multi-function workstations include provision for filing of papers, computer printouts, sound and video cassettes, and floppy discs. Specially-designed cases, trolleys, and cabinets are available for those with traditional furniture.
7. A memory-nudge file and address list can be incorporated into a word processing system and hence reduce the amount of paper space used for such items. Both files can be easily updated and modified. Their main usage would be screen based.

Short problems

1. A junior trainee secretary has just been recruited to help you in your work, which involves a great deal of correspondence and report work. You feel she could assist you in the filing of papers but your boss is loath to allow her to do this as he feels the efficient system you have established may fall apart. In order to persuade him, what advantages could you put forward and how would you suggest the junior should be trained?
2. For any secretary taking over a new job it is important that her predecessor should leave her some handover notes about the job. You are about to start a new post. What sort of information would you expect to have been left about the filing system you will have to operate and why?

Suggested solution to problem 1

What would be the direct advantages from your boss's point of view?
- Would ensure that someone else is capable of operating the system efficiently when you are absent — particularly useful during holiday periods and sickness.
- Could guarantee that filing is always up to date and there would never be a backlog, which could occur when you were exceptionally busy.
- If you move on, someone else is trained.

What would be the advantages from your point of view?
- Would eventually reduce your routine filing tasks, giving you more time to devote to specialized work.
- Would enable you to consider and introduce any refinements necessary to improve the system even further.

- Would be a great help at 'pruning' time.
- A second person capable of retrieving documents would increase efficiency when you were in conference.

What would be the advantages for the junior?
- Would give her a good grounding in operating an established and efficient filing system, so vital if she is to take up a secretarial post.
- Would give her a greater understanding of the job and work in hand, which should increase her interest and improve efficiency in other areas.
- Would give her a sense of continuity in the work she is undertaking.
- Filing practice would influence her development in other ways:
  - Initially, having a basic routine would give her a sense of belonging.
  - The chance to organize her own priorities and workload should encourage a sense of responsibility and increase her confidence to show initiative.
  - It should help her acquire a clear, logical approach to other work.

How would you train the junior?
- Don't give her the filing to do straight away. (Many secretaries do because they are eager to off-load the task. This is demoralizing because they are asking the junior to work with a system she won't understand.)
- Build up her confidence and the rapport between you by letting her get used to one job initially.
- When you feel she is ready and you can make it more realistic by referring to and accessing work she has done, explain the system to her and let her make notes. At the same time provide a list of files for reference purposes.
- Allow her a few days to study it and, in quiet moments, experiment accessing information.
- During the next week she should mark in pencil where she would file copies of the work she has produced. You *must* find time to check and discuss her decisions with her.
- If not already established, decide on a release-for-filing sign. You must remember to incorporate this into your work routine for papers placed in the filing tray — particularly if follow-up and pending items are also placed there.
- Let the junior assist you with the filing:
  - By taking papers from the filing tray, discussing with her which file to use and letting her mark in pencil accordingly.
  - By helping her to put them in order.
  - By encouraging her to gather equipment needed (punch, stapler) before she begins.

87

- By allowing her to place papers in the files under your supervision.
- By ensuring the maintenance of chronological order and the careful placing of papers.
- Continue in this way letting your junior take more responsibility as competence increases.
- Avoid complexities of cross-reference (if possible) until the junior is quite confident with straightforward filing.
- Do not ignore mistakes and rectify them in silence. The junior will not learn in this way. Her mistakes should be pointed out to her and a reason given why she is wrong.
- As soon as possible give her responsibility of the charge-out system and the careful monitoring of these papers.

Suggested solution to problem 2
Method
Assuming that the keys to all the filing equipment have been left for you, the first thing you need to know is the method of filing used and if this is a numerically based one, a copy of the complete index should be supplied.

If a mixture of two or more methods is in operation, then a rationale should be supplied in order to facilitate your decision-making.

A composite list of the file names should be available for you and this should also indicate cross-reference areas to avoid constant reference to the filing cabinet.

Operation
How your boss indicates that papers are ready for filing to avoid filing documents that still need action taking on them:

Those documents that are received
regularly and that can be filed
immediately   } so that your boss is
                                               not bothered with
Documents that do   unnecessary paperwork.
not need to be filed at
all

The recommended filing intervals to avoid accumulation and consequent inefficiencies.

Auxiliary systems
These include instructions regarding tickler files and pending file procedures to ensure that nothing is overlooked particularly in the immediate future. (This could also include those files needed by your boss for his appointments

during the first few days of your employment.)

Details of the provision for filing that does not fit into the standard system are needed, e.g.:

- Drawings and plans.
- Publications, computer printouts (and, because these tend to look alike, the categories or reference numbers in use).
- Floppy discs with printout of their indexes indicating the contents.

Details about personal and confidential files, their location, and any special security procedures should also be given.

Information regarding what indexing equipment is available, how it operates, and the use to which it is put will ensure that records are kept up to date.

Additional notes

The following notes will also be helpful:

- The particular idiosyncrasies of your boss regarding filing.
- The pruning and retention policy which is applied.

What additional information would you need to have if:

1. Microforms were used and filed departmentally?
2. Microforms were used and filed centrally?
3. A microfilm agency was used?
4. Papers were filed in a centralized system?

Case study

Sue Lawson works for the area sales coordinator, Jack Barcroft, in the busy sales department of an air freight company (Fig. 7.1).

As a result of a planned sales drive business is booming. The number of customers has grown and a wider range of goods is being transported to an increasing number of destinations.

This has caused a paperwork explosion and more staff have had to be employed to deal with it.

The heavily used departmental filing system to which everyone has access is breaking down. It has become muddled and consequently a great deal of time is being lost. Sue feels that a new and improved system should be introduced but has met with opposition to this suggestion from all quarters. She has, however, heard grumbling on the grapevine about the problems the current system is creating.

It is generally felt that if a change were to be made the existing filing system would be completely out of action for some time, making it impossible for the

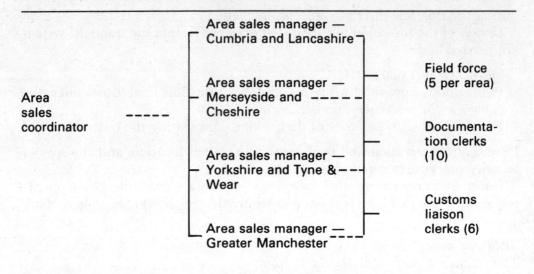

Figure 7.1 Organization chart

members of the department to carry out their work. Some people also feel that there would be teething troubles when the new system was introduced and that furthermore they would have to learn how to operate the new system which would be time-consuming.

Sue decides to speak with Jack Barcroft and he suggests that she should study and assess the utilization of the system so that her findings can be incorporated in a memo to be circulated to all sections in order to get employees' views on the subject.

What facets will Sue have to study in order to put forward a comprehensive proposal for reorganization? (You are not required to give details of the new system to be adopted.)

Her proposals were accepted in principle but members were still apprehensive about the problems that might arise during the changeover. Mr Barcroft has consequently promised that a schedule will be drawn up showing how the changeover will take place so that it will run smoothly and efficiently with the minimum of upheaval to the staff concerned. As the idea of changing the filing system came from Sue he has also given her the task of preparing this schedule.

What points will Sue have to consider before the schedule can be produced?

Produce a suitable changeover schedule

Suggested approach

1. *What facets will Sue have to study in order to put forward a comprehensive proposal for reorganization?*

   These can be basically broken down into the system itself and the usage of the system. The various facets of each element are shown in Fig. 7.2 and you should be able to enlarge upon each point made.

2. *What points will Sue have to consider before the schedule can be produced?*

   Potential user problems Because the changeover cannot take place overnight, some of the facets shown in Fig. 7.2 could equally create problems for the users during the time that the system is being rationalized and changed.

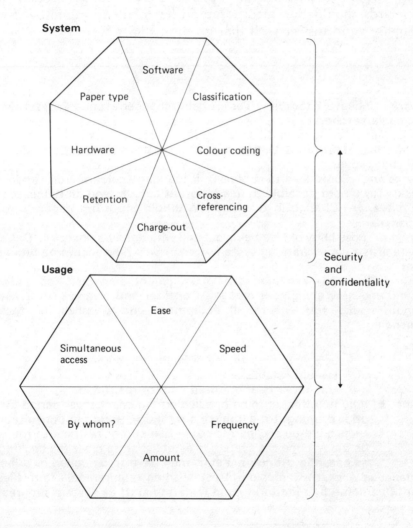

Figure 7.2   The facets of the system that Sue will have to study

Study this figure again and extract those facets that are likely to create problems before reading the list given below.

System	*Usage*
Software	Ease
Classification	Speed
Colour coding	Frequency
Cross-referencing	Amount
Charge-out system	Simultaneous access
Hardware	

What sort of problems are likely to arise in each of these sections and what safeguards should Sue incorporate in her plans to minimize disruption? Compare your answer with that given in Fig. 7.3.

System

Software   Upheaval if too many files are being changed at once. **Careful division into manageable batches.**

Classification   During reclassification staff will have to work with two systems. **Keep staff informed of progress. Limit access as far as possible to staff involved with the actual changeover.**

Colour coding   Could lead to confusion if the same colours are used for different purposes. **Try where possible to use different colours and limit access to files.**

Cross-reference   Change in emphasis. **Withhold inputting papers until system established.**

Charge-out   Possibility of files being out and whereabouts unknown. **Call in all files and establish a clear charging system. Ensure out-files accommodated into new system.**

Hardware   Changeover from one type of equipment to another. Reduced filing area while old and new equipment present. **Consider and arrange for availability of maximum space and ensure all equipment and supplies in stock before commencing.**

Usage

Ease ⎫
Speed ⎬   access to files will be difficult until complete system established.
Frequency ⎭   **Use must be monitored and/or restricted.**

Amount   ● Volume of paper to be handled during changeover period. **Reduce by prior pruning. Re-establish a retention period in consultation.**

Amount   ● Huge build-up of papers to be filed if inputting restricted. **Provision must be made once the system is established to clear the backlog as soon as possible. Additional staff may have to be called in to help.**

Simultaneous Access   Confusion in establishing requirements from files in new system. **Overcome by monitoring and updating staff as system progresses.**

Figure 7.3 Problems that might arise; their suggested solutions are shown in bold type

Organization problems So far we have only considered how to avoid the problems that might arise with other users of the system.

What tasks will Sue have to undertake to ensure that problems do not crop up for herself and her helpers once the changeover is in full swing?

The keywords below should give you a clue:

Delivery dates   *Stock of supplies*   *List of files*   *Timetable*
Use of microfilm?   *Increased fire hazards and security risks*   *Archival boxes*

3. *Produce a suitable schedule*

Analyse all the points raised together with the safeguards to be taken and put them into a working plan. A time-scale can then be added.

What should be the last jobs to be done by Sue once the changeover has been accomplished to ensure that the new system operates efficiently from the start?

She should prepare a complete list of files for distribution to all concerned to ensure that papers are correctly identified when released for filing and to facilitate accessing of information.

One step further

How would you advise Sue to ensure that the new standard departmental filing system was well-maintained?

Long problem

A close family friend, who is a qualified surveyor, valuer, and estate agent, has approached you about the possibility of going into partnership with him to run an estate agency in the Midlands town where you live. It is envisaged that he would run the technical side of the business and you would be involved in the organization of the office and the running of the 'front desk'. He is well known in the area and therefore has a great many contacts for setting up a residential properties business. All properties on the books will be within a radius of 15 miles.

You are most interested in the idea and, after looking at a string of potential offices, you have found one to rent in a prime position. This will, however, involve the investment of a high percentage of available capital, making — for the time being at least — the purchase of any sophisticated electronic equipment impossible.

With regard to the filing system you will operate you have made a list of those files you feel you will need to keep. This is shown in Fig. 7.4.

Vendors	– Details of houses to give to potential clients. Brief details to put in window. Confidential files for each vendor to maintain correspondence.
Potential purchases	– Quick method of getting details of properties they require. Mailing list of future properties. Follow-up system.
Purchases	– Details when offer made – keep on card index?
Other files needed	– Photographer, solicitor, press, professional associations, insurance, council billing system.
General office files	– Maintenance of equipment, stationery supplies, cleaning, running expenses, etc.

Figure 7.4   Your list of files you will need to keep

There are sufficient funds for the purchase of necessary furniture, lateral or vertical filing cabinets, a desk-top copier, and any other ancillary equipment that may be required.

Tasks:
1. Decide on a suitable system for filing the vendors' files and details.
2. Devise a quick access system to provide potential purchasers with details of properties on your books. How will this be tied up with the window display?
3. How will you ensure that potential purchasers are informed of any new suitable properties?
4. How will you record actual purchasers while negotiations are in progress?
5. How will you indicate ongoing changes in the status of the property, e.g.: when it has been advertised? Siting and updating of the 'For Sale' boards? If the price is reduced? When it is under offer?
6. Will you make any provision for retaining details of properties sold?
7. What method will you use for the other files you need to keep?

Suggested approach

It must be appreciated that, as with so many other organizational problems, there is no one correct answer and, by contacting several estate agents in your district, you will realize that there is no one standard system adopted by estate agents in general.

Possibilities are given for each task so that you can choose which you think would be the most appropriate. You should, however, ensure that, as far as possible, there are no loop-holes in your system and that there is a logical link between the different aspects to be considered.

Vendors' files
- Alphabetically by zone and street.
- Alphabetically by name of vendor.
- Subject by type of property.
- Numerically — last in, next number.
- Numerically by zone and last in sequence.
- Numerically by price category.

Quick access
- Edge-punched cards } to refer back to details in the file.
- Cardex system
- Self-service by price and other category in the shop area.
- Visible edge index.
- Colour coding on the outside of the vendors' files.
- Window display — card giving brief details, reference, and identifying code.

Potential purchasers
- Initially put in day-book — details entered as prospective clients come in or telephone.
- Initially list on specially designed forms — insert details of property descriptions taken or sent.
- Transfer to mailing list — cards, strip index.
- Cross-reference to quick access card/vendors' files.

Actual purchasers
- Separate card index — showing current address, phone number, and other relevant details such as solicitor, surveyor, building society.
- Details in vendor's file.

Ongoing changes
- Details on checklist in vendor's file.
- Colour coding on cards and in window display.

Retention
- Master file containing brief details of all properties sold.
- Microfilming via agency.

Other files
- Alphabetically by subject.

One step further

If you had been able to purchase some electronic equipment, what would you have chosen and how would you have incorporated it into your system?

Additional problems

1. A manufacturing company has opened a new sales office and warehouse in your town and you have secured the job of secretary to the Sales Manager. Six representatives are employed and four products are marketed. You have been asked to organize an efficient filing system. Give your suggestions.

2. As secretary to the Managing Director of a rapidly expanding travel agency, you are asked by your employer to organise a changeover from the present departmental filing systems to a centralised filing system. What actions would you take? (LCC PSC DIP)

3. Your employer runs an employment agency. The work handled is growing rapidly, with new applicants and employers being registered daily. The present filing system, where all files — current and non-current — are grouped alphabetically in filing cabinets, is proving inadequate. Explain, with reasons, what changes you would suggest. (LCC PSC)

8

It's knowing where to look

Knowledge is of two kinds. We know a subject ourselves, or we know where we can find information upon it.
JOHNSON (1709-1784)

We all gather information wittingly or unwittingly, from a variety of sources, every day of our lives. We read newspapers, listen to the radio at home or in the car, and we watch TV. We are entertained, made aware, become curious, annoyed, amused, enlightened, even educated, and are no doubt better informed than many of our forebears. The media have shrunk the world and as a result, we are more knowledgeable about many countries and many subjects.

As well as newspapers for current affairs, we read magazines according to our interests and we use reference books according to our needs.

The telephone directory is in constant use as are the *Yellow Pages* when we want to find specialists of one kind or another.

A dictionary is a constant companion if we like crosswords, can't spell, or just enjoy words! A *Roget's Thesaurus* is a must if we are writing a report, a letter, or even an essay and have used the same word umpteen times. We may even have a well-worn copy of *Hartrampf's Vocabularies*.

'Where' more important than 'what'
In whatever business you find yourself, you, as a secretary, should know *where* to look for the information you need in your particular job. This is far more realistic than trying to retain the facts which, in any event, are subject to change.

There is a great wealth of information available, from a wide variety of sources, to help the businessman run his business and while it may be difficult to keep up to date, it will be invaluable if you regularly read the relevant trade magazines, keep in touch with your local reference library, and are aware of new services offered.

Many county and large city or urban reference libraries have a commercial

97

information service and it is our experience that the librarians will go to no end of trouble in helping one to solve a particular problem or they may even solve it themselves!

Find out

There is no doubt that browsing through specific books will enable you to become more knowledgeable and, in order to find out what is available on your particular topic area, you may find it interesting to thumb through:

The Aslib Directory Vol. I (information sources in science and technology, in Great Britain and Ireland)
Facts at Your Fingertips by K. G. Harrison
Facts and How to Find Them by W. Bagley
How to Find Out by G. Chandler.

You may even find your own library stocks additional books of this kind.

All reference books are regularly updated either by the publication of a new edition or by means of supplements supplied to subscribers as and when information changes. (If you haven't discovered, for example, the *Croner* publications and the *Employment Law Manual,* among others, you will surely know the *Post Office Guide* and *British Telecom Guide.*

Company information is available from Kompass of Croydon (all EEC countries and others including Australia and Switzerland) and services or organizations such as Extel Statistical Services Limited and Dun & Bradstreet. The Companies Register in Cardiff produces information in the form of microfiche (able to be copied in some libraries where reader/printers are available), which are updated every month as new companies are registered and old ones fall by the wayside.

Using the press

Newspapers are a valuable reference source and have the great advantage of being the most up to date of all published media. The *Financial Times* is considered to be compulsory reading by many businessmen and their secretaries may be asked to study it and extract or precis articles and information of particular interest.

Magazines and trade journals are also current, may be specialized, and can be chosen to fulfil your particular needs. For instance, the rapid changes in office technology have made it more essential for secretaries to try to keep abreast of developments and be well informed. Help can be found in such publications as:

Business Information Technology (a new publication with articles written in a style that is easily understood by the layman)
Business Equipment and News } (Magazines packed with information
Business Equipment Digest } on latest products)
Better buys for Business (aimed at helping the businessman to choose, when a particular need has been identified)

You may read *Memo* or *2000*, or even *Office Skills*, and these contain some very useful and interesting articles to keep both student and teacher up to date.

In the library that was the subject of our study, a current awareness file is kept of articles taken out of newspapers and magazines and then classified and indexed. A daily press sheet is also produced giving details of articles and their sources and of which photocopies are available if required.

If, in your own line of business, you are not aware of the periodicals available, you may find it useful to consult a guide to current periodicals. *British Union Catalogue* is a list of periodicals both past and present and where they may be located. *Ulrich's International Periodicals* provides a current list of published periodicals.

Other sources

An important aid to finding up-to-date information is *The Research Index,* a comprehensive reference to articles and news items of financial and business interest which have appeared in over 100 periodicals and the national press during the previous fortnight.

The Reports Index published every two months by Business Surveys Limited lists recent reports and available sources classified under section headings. This makes fascinating reading.

A variety of terms have been used to describe screen-based information sources but an apt one seems to be that used in the magazine, *Business Information Technology* —'Business TV'. This falls mainly into two categories:

1. *Telext* — used to describe the broadcast television information services offered by BBC 1's Ceefax I, BBC 2's Ceefax II, and ITV's Oracle which are of more limited use than other systems because the process is one way, the number of pages is restricted, and the access to pages is by rotation. However, information costs nothing, useful business information is available, and future developments using cable TV systems as in use in the USA, will allow two-way communication.

2. *Viewdata* — used to describe systems that transmit data over the public telephone network and allow the user to have interaction through the use of respond frames. The best known system in the UK is Prestel — British Telecom's public service.

Information providers are licensed to create data (as well as the information carrier). Frames may be charged for and some are relatively expensive.

Not all pages are available for the general public. A group of users can pay to be a 'closed user group' (in which case the pages controlled by the group are available only to members of that group who gain access by special security codes).

With the advent of Gateway, it is possible for Prestel users to have access, by retrieval of a Gateway page, to many databases and host systems. This will clearly extend computer services to a greater number of users.

As the final word on business TV, mention must be made of private viewdata systems that provide individual businesses with their own specially tailored Prestel-like system. They are considered to offer a cost-effective means of installing proper electronic mail systems as well as providing an ideal general in-house information and current awareness system.

In conclusion

Attempt the end, and never stand to doubt;
Nothing's so hard, but search will find it out.

ROBERT HERRICK (1591-1674)

This must surely be the maxim of reference section librarians. The vast amount of reference books and sources available in the commercial section alone is not only overwhelming but also intriguing to the layman. What is more, it provides such a tremendous back-up system that the likelihood of anyone being faced with an insoluble problem, must be extremely low.

While it may be possible to have the research carried out by the librarians, there is nevertheless a fascination and an increased sense of achievement in solving the problem oneself. It may take a little time but then 'the true success is to labour' (*Stevenson:* 1850-1894).

We hope that once you have tackled the problems presented in this chapter, you too will eagerly accept such research challenges in the future, content in the knowledge that you and every other citizen are provided with the back-up support of our public libraries.

We certainly owe our grateful thanks to Gloucestershire County Library's Commercial Service staff at Cheltenham Reference Library for all their time, effort, and, above all, patience. *Our very special thanks to Miss E. Loder FLA, reference librarian.*

Do you know

1. What such reference books as *Roget's Thesaurus, Who's Who, Pear's Cyclopaedia, Whitaker's Almanack,* and *Kelly's Directories* are and how to use them?
2. Which trade journals are published relating to the particular type of industry in which you are interested?
3. How to use the indexing system in your local library?
4. How to use one or more of the business TV systems available?
5. What services are offered by bureaux and agencies specializing in travel, employment, secretarial services, printing, translating, microfilming, computing, word processing, market research, advertising, importing and exporting, and industrial and financial consultancy?

Snippets

1. Extel cards produced by Exchange Telegraph Statistics Services Ltd give information on British public and major private companies quoted on the Stock Exchange. The service includes an annual card giving full details of each company, updated by a news card containing current information. Unquoted company cards are also produced and are usually held in the major city libraries.
2. An Extel card is also produced giving cost of living indices for the last five years and an index of retail prices for a number of countries.
3. Lloyds Bank regularly produces economic reports for most countries, as do Barclay's International. In addition their economic intelligence units collect information and monitor situations, but these units cannot be approached directly by the public.
4. The British Overseas Trade Board (BOTB) produces a booklet, *BOTB's Services,* which gives details of all of the services available to help British exporters and is essential for any business wishing to export.
5. BOTB publishes *Hints to Exporters* — a series of booklets on 100 overseas markets. *Business Traveller's handbook* published by Michael Joseph also aims to help businessmen overseas.
6. The Statistics and Market Intelligence Library (SMIL) in London is provided by the government to supply published information on overseas markets. Reports from foreign counties are available. Ten-year plans for those countries are kept by SMIL but may be loaned out.
7. The Small Firm's Information Service is offered by the Department of Industry to enable businessmen to receive advice and guidance. It is on the mailing list of most embassies and they send notification of goods to be made under licence, which may be circulated by local offices to likely firms in the area.
8. *British Business* gives weekly news from the Department of Industry and Trade and has a supplement twice a year on trade fairs and produces a trade promotions guide.
9. The British Library is one of the largest and most comprehensive in the world and has the right to receive a free copy of every book published in the UK. British Library Automated Information Service (BLAISE) provides a databank of bibliographical information for the use of libraries and organizations subscribing to the system.

101

10. The British Institute of Management Foundation (BIM) provides a free reference library and information service to the general public. Collective subscription to the institute is essential, however, to take advantage of the full library service and to receive details of reading lists provided on a variety of management topics and various BIM publications that are provided to members either free of charge or at a reduced rate. The institute also produces a monthly journal — *Management Today* — and a quarterly publication — *Management Review and Digest*. The management information centre contains one of the largest management libraries in the world.

11. Information retrieval systems provide access to information held on external databases. British Telecom International provides facilities for access to Diane (Direct Information Access Network for Europe). This is an on-line information retrieval service, which is available to subscribers through the data communications network for Europe (Euronet).

Short problems

1. Your boss has been scratching his head over a couple of speeches he has been asked to give. One is for an Anglo-American political dinner and the other is for a diamond wedding celebration. He is anxious to quote from Churchill in his speech at the dinner and he believes there is a quotation in which he remembers something about 'the British Empire and the United States being mixed up in each other's affairs'. For the diamond wedding speech he seems to recall a line about 'breakfast-time being a tricky period' and he would like to quote this and the origin if possible. Can you help him?

2. Many reference books do not contain up-to-the-minute information. What exceptions are there to this statement? What other sources might help you to find up-to-date information? (LCC PSC)

Suggested solution to problem 1

There are a number of dictionaries of quotations and the *Oxford Dictionary of Quotations* is very comprehensive. If the author is known, as in the first example, the quotation may be located by reading through all of the quotations listed for that author. Alternatively, a very full index is provided in the last third of the book and the quotations in both instances may be located by looking up the keywords *British Empire* and *Breakfast period*.

Suggested solution to problem 2

Exceptions

Since many reference books are published annually, the information may become out of date as the year goes by. Exceptions to this are those to which supplements are issued to all subscribers when information changes. Among these are:

- The various *Croner* reference books, e.g., for exporters, importers, and small businesses.
- the *Employment Law Manual* — updated by supplements giving the latest developments in legislation and case law and implications for management practice.
- *Palmer's Company Law and the Law relating to Trade Descriptions.*
- *Post Office Guide* — supplements are issued when rates are changed at home or overseas.
- *Hansard* gives official daily reports of proceedings in Parliament.
- *Keesing's Contemporary Archives* are weekly sheets of international news abstracted from the world's press and news information service.
- Her Majesty's Stationery Office provides an index of retail prices and statistics on manpower, wages, etc.
- *The Research Index* is published fortnightly.
- *BRAD* (British Rate and Data) is a monthly guide for advertisers.
- Dictionaries and other etymological sources; ready reckoners; atlases.

Other sources
Newspapers and magazines
Financial Times gives share prices and rates of exchange; *Daily Telegraph* and its information bureau; *Guardian, Observer, The Times* for special reports, leaders, obituaries, etc; trade magazines. *Economic Trends.* Her Majesty's Stationery Office publications.

Travel
Travel agencies; airlines; British Rail; AA or RAC handbooks.

Organizations
Department of Trade and Industry; Department of Health and Social Security; Economist Intelligence Unit; EEC Information Service; embassies and trade delegations; United Nations London Information Centre; London Chamber of Commerce Research Information Department; British Overseas Boards; British Standards Institution; specialist and professional organizations and institutions, e.g., Institute of Linguists, British Institute of Managers; motoring organizations.

Local
Local council planning office; banks; citizens advice bureau; consumer research bureau; local chamber of commerce; tax offices; reference libraries;

agencies — employment, press cutting, market research; local independent radio; specialist libraries; telephone services including directory enquiries; probably one of the most important sources of up-to-date information is business TV; databases.

This is a much fuller answer than we believe would be expected in an examination. Nevertheless, the list of sources is not considered to be exhaustive.

Short problems

Below are some problems that could be presented in any secretarial job. The information is available from the sources listed below; the list is not exhaustive. Using the appropriate sources, find answers to all of the problems.

1. From whom do you obtain an import licence for potatoes?
2. Obtain a list of subsidiaries of Unilever in Canada.
3. How would you locate the latest accounts and report from Debenhams with recent articles?
4. What is the address of the manufacturers of 'Radicon'?
5. What is the cost of a letter telegram to the Cayman Islands?
6. What is the registered address of Harcourt Public Relations Ltd?
7. Find the latest unemployment figures with regional breakdowns.
8. Locate any recent reports on office equipment.
9. Where would you obtain the percentage forecast figures for retail sales by type of organization for the next three years?
10. Is it possible to send a coded telegram to Saudi Arabia?
11. When are the public holidays in French Guiana?
12. How much would it cost to send a parcel weighing 10 kg to the Azores by airmail?
13. What are the latest FT index figures?
14. Find the statistics for wage rates and earnings over the last 10 years to include the present year.
15. Find the address of the dustbin makers, Judge International.
16. What is BS 1589?
17. Where would you find the cost of living index for last five years?
18. Prepare a list of giftware and jewellery trade fairs in England and Italy for the next year.
19. You are doing a French translation and have come across the initials RFA. What do they mean?
20. What are the development grant regulations?

Sources

Business Surveys Reports Index
Business Surveys Research Index
Britain – a handbook
British Telecom Guide
British Standards Yearbook
Ceefax
Companies Registration
Croner's Exporters
Croner's Importers
Delmas French Business Directory
Economic Trends

Extel cards
Monthly Digest of Statistics
Hints to exporters
Kompass
Post Office Guide
Prestel Government Statistics
The Exhibitor's Handbook
UK Trade Names
Who Owns Whom
Retail Trade in the UK

Long problem

The company for which you work manufactures toys that are distributed at present under their own trade name to wholesale toy specialists throughout the UK. It is the policy of the board to extend the company's activities by importing toys possibly from Scandinavia, Taiwan, India, and Germany and retailing direct by high street shops throughout the whole of the country. A pilot scheme will be set up in the south-east region.

As personal assistant to the managing director you have been asked to set up an in-company library of reference books and other sources that will assist the managing director, marketing director, and purchasing director and their staff in their negotiations. Also included in your brief is an investigation into the various agencies and outside sources that could be of assistance to set this up. You are to work on an initial budget of £3000 (excluding the fittings and fixtures) with £1000 per annum thereafter to keep the reference sources you have established up to date. It is envisaged that you will be promoted to the post of information officer once you have received the necessary training to run such a service.

Tasks

1. Investigate suitable books, journals, and other reference sources:
   (a) To aid the importation of the toys — don't forget a considerable amount of travel will be involved.
   (b) To aid the marketing of these toys.
2. What types of agency and other outside sources would you feel could be useful to your organization in the purchasing and/or marketing of the products?

3. Produce a statement to show how you would spend your allocated budget both for setting up the library and as an on-going reference service. You should be able to justify the purchase of each item.

Suggested approach

1. To aid the importation of the toys, sources are needed that will:

- Give information of companies and countries manufacturing certain categories of toys.
- Give information on the countries of origin.
- Aid communication with these countries.
- Give economic trends about the worldwide toy industry.
- Provide details of safety regulations for new categories of toys to be stocked.
- Provide information on import procedures, documents required, etc.
- Enable you to make travel arrangements and investigate freight methods and availability.

2. To aid the marketing of the toys sources are needed that will:

- Identify suitable areas — local information.
- Give trends on sales of toys in the UK.
- Provide suitable marketing methods as the company is new to direct retailing, e.g., promotions, fairs, advertising, training sessions.
- Provide company information — may possibly have to set up subsidiary company to market the goods.
- Ensure foreign goods are marketable — name and instructions, presentation.

Investigations of the above points should have identified the advisability of using some outside specialist agencies and sources — at least in the initial stages.

Once you have earmarked the sources you could use, reconsider them with cost factors in mind.

One step further

Choose a suitable topic or topics of interest to yourself and, over the next few months, set up your own current awareness file, complete with index. Use as wide a range of periodicals and newspapers, plus any other sources, as you can.

Part Four

Keeping it safe

9

A potentially dangerous environment

A chapter of accidents.
CHESTERFIELD (1694-1773)

As you read the title to this part of the book you may well have thought 'Here we go again on the same old safety problems'. But does 'keeping it safe' mean only that? Not in our view. There are now several areas emerging in secretarial work that are being recognized as having importance in this field. What is perhaps more important to you if you are a student is that examining bodies are also picking up the relevance of these aspects and bringing in topics that involve problem-solving on these subjects.

The reasons for this increase in importance are manifold but include:

- The introduction of the Health and Safety at Work Act 1974.
- The wider use of advanced technology, which was previously the province of the specialist.
- The easy transmission of information to all parts of the world.
- Increased quantities of stored documents.

Although it must be remembered that they are closely interrelated, this section can be broken down into three main headings:

Safety   *Security*   *Confidentiality*

The first chapter covers those points that you will already have dealt with when learning legislation affecting safety in the office and all its implications.

The second two areas are not, however, so easily defined because the maintenance of security means that confidentiality is also maintained, and vice versa.

As you are aware, the 1974 Health and Safety at Work Act sets out the basic obligations of employers to safeguard, as far as is reasonably practicable, the health, safety, and welfare of the people who work for them.

The Act also places basic obligations on employees to act with care for the health and safety of themselves, other workers, and the general public.

This is the first time the legal responsibility for their own safety has been put on the *workers* as well as onto the employers.

How does this affect you as a secretary?

Large company   You could find yourself elected as the safety representative of your department and, as such, you would be expected to be aware of the hazards in the different sections and be able to recommend how these could be minimized. It would be your responsibility to make your colleagues safety conscious and aware of their responsibilities in the search for safety within the office.

Small company   Here your safety role may not be so clearly defined but you are nevertheless your employer's representative and, as well as being responsible for yourself, you must be well informed with regard to the provisions of the Act: be vigilant, regarding hazards, and organize regular checks on the overall working environment.

Developing safety consciousness   In our view, it is essential that new employees have the safety aspect of the job and the environment in which they will work incorporated into their induction programme and that juniors be adequately supervised by competent personnel, at least in the initial stages.

Safety consciousness can also be achieved by the use of dramatic notices, slogans, and cartoons. Remember, however, that these need to be changed frequently to ensure that they are, in fact, 'noticed'.

Horrific films too can make an impact by locating the hidden dangers in the office environment:

- The metal waste paper bin into which lighted cigarettes are thrown.
- The vertical filing cabinet with drawers left open.
- The plate-glass doors that swing both ways.
- The untidy desk concealing potentially dangerous weapons.
- The multitude of electrical hazards.

Hazardous behaviour   It should be borne in mind, however, that it is not only inanimate objects that are dangerous. These can be controlled; but people are often a hazard both to themselves and to others. How many times have you seen a person carrying so many files or books that he cannot see where he is going? Or what about latecomers to the office, all trying to crowd into the lift designed to carry only four people?

It is your duty to call attention to such behaviour.

Do you know?

1. The original requirements of the Offices, Shops, and Railways Premises Act 1963, which has been incorporated into, and not superseded by, the Health and Safety at Work Act 1974?
2. The correct way to lift any large item of equipment should you require to move it?

110

3. The exact location of your nearest fire extinguisher, fire exit, and fire drill notice at this moment?
4. Where and how to report any accidents that may occur?

Snippets

1. In calculating the number of employees for the provision of first-aid boxes under the Factories Act, three office workers count as one manual worker.
2. Typical contents of a first-aid box must include: form SHW1 (*Advice on First-Aid Treatment*); small, medium, and large sterilized unmedicated finger dressings; assorted sizes of adhesive wound dressings; a triangular bandage; 1" adhesive plaster; $\frac{1}{2}$ oz packets of absorbent sterilized cotton wool; sterilized eye pads; safety pins; rubber bandages.
3. The Health and Safety at Work Act 1974 is constantly being updated and it is anticipated that companies will be asked to have more trained first-aiders and better first-aid facilities, always in accordance with their particular business. In addition, the ratio of front-line first-aiders to employees is to be increased.
4. The British Safety Council offers membership for approximately £25 per annum. In return companies receive the Council's monthly magazine, are provided with details of courses for safety representatives and first-aid, and can obtain the many effective posters published by the Council.
5. At the annual general meeting of any company the director's annual report must, by law, include information relating to health and safety matters.
6. Office workers sustain more than 5000 injuries per year and this includes only those that necessitate absence from work for more than three days. A far higher figure would be reached if minor bumps, cuts, and abrasions were included.
7. The British Standards Institution specifies an internationally recognized system for giving health or safety information that keeps the use of words to a minimum. The purpose of a system of safety colours and safety signs is to draw attention to objects and situations that affect or could affect health or safety. These became mandatory in 1981 under an EEC directive (see Fig. 9.1, page 112).

Short problems

Construct separate instructional notices to ensure that accidents do not occur with regard to:

- Trailing wires.
- Vertical filing cabinets.
- Electrically-operated equipment.

Suggested solutions

These appear in Figs 9.2 (page 112), 9.3 (page 113), and 9.4 (page 114).

Safety colour	Meaning or purpose	Examples of use	Contrasting colour (if required)	Symbol
Red*	Stop Prohibition	Stop signs. Identification and colour of emergency shutdown devices. Prohibition signs.	White	
Yellow	Caution, risk of danger	Indication of hazards (fire, explosion, radiation, chemical, etc.) Warning signs. Identification of thresholds, dangerous passages, obstacles.	Black	
Blue	Mandatory action	Obligation to wear personal safety equipment. Mandatory signs.	White	
Green	Safe condition	Identification of safety showers, first-aid posts and rescue points. Emergency exit signs.	White	

* Red is also used to identify fire fighting equipment and its location.

Figure 9.1   Table of safety colours and contrasting colours. (From BS 5378:Part 1:1980, specification for Safety Colours and Safety Signs). Reproduced by permission of the British Standards Institution, 2 Park Street, London W1A 2BS

1. Use the nearest power point.
2. Do not move the telephone around the office when talking on it.
3. Keep doorways and gangways free from trailing wires.
4. Keep cables off desk surfaces.
5. Move yourself to the machinery, not the machinery to you!
6. Wind cable neatly when finished with machine, and neatly clamp excessive cable length.

Figure 9.2   Trailing wires

1. Open only one drawer at a time.
2. Ensure an even spread of files throughout the cabinet.
3. Close all drawers after use.
4. Beware of sharp edges.

Figure 9.3   Vertical filing cabinets

Only open one drawer at a time

1. Do not overload electrical sockets.
2. Check and report any broken plug casings or loose wiring.
3. Switch on at the mains before switching on equipment.
4. Switch off and unplug after use and always at the end of the day.
5. Hold the plug, not the cable, when removing from sockets.

Figure 9.4   Electrically-operated machines

Do not overload electric sockets

Long problem

There has been an increase in the number of accidents in the small but busy firm of solicitors for which you work. It would appear that most of them were caused by a lack of care and attention.

Your employer, the senior partner, has asked you to draw up a set of rules for the prevention of accidents for distribution to all employees and mentioning several incidents of hazardous behaviour that have been noticed recently.

Suggested approach
1. Identify specific danger areas:
    (a) What are the main areas of movement? Any obstructions?
    (b) Is there any potentially dangerous equipment?
    (c) Is there a potential fire hazard?
2. Identify preventive measures:
    (a) Is the area of movement adequate for the number of people?
    (b) Are maintenance and repair facilities adequate?
    (c) What fire prevention measures are there?
3. Identify remaining causes of accidents:
    (a) Are accidents being caused by thoughtlessness and carelessness?
    (b) Are employees not accepting their responsibility to prevent accidents happening?

Now that you have investigated all areas, you should be able to put your ideas down in the form of rules. Before you look at Fig. 9.5 (page 116), try to write your own set of rules.

One step further
Assuming that you have identified all possible danger areas, let us set the scene in the office where you work.

It is an old building, your office is on the second floor, has a high ceiling, and is square with one tall window overlooking the busy street below. The window faces south. Although there is a ladies' toilet on your floor, cloakroom facilities are on the floor below, which encourages the leaving of coats and bags in the office. Five people work in the office and you are equipped with wooden desks, electric typewriters, and metal filing cabinets. Plug sockets are in the walls at skirting board level, lighting is from a chandelier-type lamp, and the floor is covered with an ill-fitting carpet. Altogether a dreary prospect!

Produce a report for your employer indicating how the room could be improved to make it a pleasant hazard-free area without spending a great deal of money.

Long problem
You work for a small company that buys, strips, and restores antique furniture. You are secretary to the general manager who has asked you to investigate what seems to be an outbreak of a skin infection among employees. How would you go about this?

Do:
- Use the hooks and cloakroom facilities provided for all personal possessions.
- Use the nearest plug point (without overloading the socket).
- When moving typewriters, lock the carriage and carry with the back towards your body.
- Pass scissors with the handle towards the person *receiving* them.
- When smoking in de-restricted areas, use the ashtrays provided and ensure that you stub the cigarette out completely.
- Switch off all electrical appliances when leaving the office.
- Keep to the right on stairs and corridors.
- Ensure that you know the position of the first-aid boxes in the office.
- Use emergency switches if machinery jams or gives any cause for concern and call the technician immediately.
- Keep all fire doors closed even if you feel more air is needed in the office.
- Ensure that you know where the fire escapes are situated and what the fire drill is.
- Turn off taps in all washrooms.
- Keep flammable or reflecting materials away from full sun.
- Keep your work area tidy so that there are no hidden dangers.
- *Report any hazards or hazardous behaviour to your safety representative.*

Don't:
- Leave shopping bags or handbags in the aisles between desks.
- Try and repair electrical equipment yourself.
- Use an electric typewriter that is emitting unusual noises.
- Strike matches or use a cigarette lighter near correcting fluid or inflammable liquids.
- Obscure fire extinguishers.
- Trail wires across the office — electrical or telephone.
- Try and carry anything that is too heavy for you.
- Smoke in restricted areas.
- Hang mobiles near light fittings.
- Leave electric appliances switched on when the office is unattended.
- Gather for discussion in narrow corridors, in the reception area, or on landings.
- Run down corridors.
- Carry a stack of books or files that make it difficult to see where you are going.
- Remove stickers from plate-glass doors.
- Exceed the stated number of people in the lift.

Figure 9.5 General safety rules

Suggested approach

This is a potentially illegal situation in so far as the cause of the suspected skin infection may be as a result of conditions that contravene the Health and Safety at Work Act.

Before reading on you should work out what initial information you would need before you could go any further.

1. Who are the people suffering from the skin infection? Is it everyone or just people on the shop floor?
2. Analyse the various jobs they undertake; is everyone involved in the whole process?
3. Once you have gleaned these facts, you should consult with your boss on the need for obtaining a medical report from the Employment Medical Advisor in your area, and having any tests done that may be necessary.
4. *If the tests indicate the cause to be the materials used*
   (a) Are employees following manufacturers' instructions?
   (b) Is adequate protective clothing provided and being used?
   (c) If occasional accidents are unavoidable, notices informing employees of the immediate curative measures to be taken should be displayed in prominent places.
   (d) Thought should be given to the appropriateness of the contents of the first-aid box to cope with such emergencies.
   (e) Consider whether employees are adequately screened before they undertake the work. There are many advanced techniques for screening workers to find out if they react or are allergic to particular chemicals. In addition these tests can be carried out at regular intervals to ensure that what would otherwise be imperceptible changes are not creeping in to cause future problems.
5. *If tests indicate a transmissible disease*
   What would you check up? Produce a short checklist before reading on.
   (a) Can the medical practitioner identify the source and then advise on medication?
   (b) Can the means of transmitting the disease be identified?
   (c) Has each employee his own protective clothing or are overalls interchangeable?
   (d) Are cloakroom facilities adequate to prevent the transmission of disease — soap dispenser? Blow dryers not towels?
   (e) Are cloakrooms cleaned thoroughly at regular intervals?

Whatever the outcome of these investigations, your boss would have to be kept informed at all stages so that you can act on his instructions.

It could well be a situation that would involve you in the exercising of a great deal of tact and diplomacy with employees, particularly if the facilities provided were in any way to blame for the outbreak. The investigations would have to be carried out with due care and attention to reduce the risk of hysterical reaction to such a problem.

This is a very general approach to the subject as the assumptions one could make are infinite and a serious assumption could well lead one into the realms of industrial relations, tribunals, and compensation.

One step further

Investigations proved that employees involved in the stripping and cleaning process had not been wearing the protective clothing provided. Up to this point the company had had no official safety representative. It was decided to appoint one and you were elected. How would you ensure:

- An efficient system of dealing with accidents?
- That as far as possible no such outbreak occurred again?
- That you encouraged personnel to maintain as safe a working environment as possible?

10

Taking precautions

Plots, true or false, are necessary things,
to raise up commonwealths and ruin kings.

DRYDEN (1631-1700)

What is meant by security in the office and to what extent is it the responsibility of the secretary? This is a very broad question indeed.

Interpretation

In simple terms security in the office means taking precautions against the theft of anything belonging to the organization or to individuals working for or visiting the company. As well as material possessions, precautions must be taken against the theft of information about the company or about individuals. Employees in the personnel department of a large company or having access to personal files in a small company must be very carefully selected.

Information of a highly personal nature whether, for example, regarding the marital status of the person in question, or concerned with performance appraisals for career advancement, could be used very detrimentally even in terms of office gossip.

Spying!

In this age of highly competitive markets, even the smallest of companies runs the risk of industrial espionage. Information can be transmitted to competitors on a variety of aspects — the design of new products; prices; component suppliers; sales contracts and contacts; know-how; number of personnel; production capacity; expansion (or contraction); and many more.

Information can even be gained by outsiders having access to a firm's premises. A quick glance at the shop floor can tell an expert a lot. Computers present one of the greatest security risks and anyone with expertise, gaining access to a computer department, could obtain valuable information about the company. All of this would be damaging and could even destroy a company.

119

Responsibility — the James Bond role?

The extent to which security is the responsibility of the secretary will depend in great part on the size of the company.

In a very large company special personnel will be employed to manage the general security — screening all visitors, checking all buildings after staff have left to ensure that no undesirables are hidden on the premises, and possibly keeping a 24-hour CCTV surveillance of the premises.

However, even in the large company someone has to decide on security points in the first place and very often managers will be asked to make recommendations about their particular department or section. Therefore the secretary may be involved on a one-off basis when a new security procedure is being instigated and subsequently when periodic checks are made regarding the effectiveness of these precautions.

In a small company the situation could be very different. If security personnel are not employed, then it is up to the staff in general to maintain security and staff should be reminded at regular intervals of this responsibility.

Commonsense precautions

Whether you work in a large or a small company, a lot of commonsense precautions should be taken to ensure that the office is secure:

- Lock all windows and doors at night and during the day if the office is to be left unattended.
- Check the premises at the end of the day.
- Do not leave personal property lying around.
- Ensure strict reception procedures both in and out.
- Keys should be handled discriminately.
- Personnel responsible for access to confidential information should be carefully screened and the number restricted. (The American system even checks out the wives of men about to take on responsible jobs and such checking out is not unknown in Britain).
- Files should not be left lying around and all discarded paper should be shredded or burnt.
- Lockable, flameproof filing cabinets should be installed.
- If a second 'set' of records is to be kept, it is wise to use a different location.
- Word processors and computers also present new security problems. Core material and other media are of great value and should not be put at risk. Floppy discs may look innocuous but could contain a great deal of vital and confidential information. They should therefore be carefully locked away.
- Strange faces should be queried — no matter how stupid you may feel.

Increased technology makes for more refined criminals. Therefore security precautions should be refined to combat crime.

Do you know?
1. What security steps should be taken in the reception area?
2. What services security companies can provide to the small and large company?
3. The steps to take if you are faced with a bomb scare?
4. That word processors are useless without their special starter program (disc or tape). What security measures should be adopted to prevent unauthorized use of the machines?

Snippets
1. Security devices are being increasingly used, particularly in large companies, to restrict the access of unauthorized personnel to rooms containing confidential information. Gone are the days of authorized personnel simply having a key to the room in question. There are now many devices that electronically recognize the authorized person:
   (a) Magnetically-coded cards are available for insertion in a reader affixed to the door to be entered, combined with a keyboard for punching out the personal codes (compare with banking service cards/cashpoint cards). As this personal number is retained only in the person's head, it cannot be lost — only forgotten!
   (b) Security doors are fitted with a keyboard. In order to enter, a pass number has to be tapped out. There is a different pass number for each door and these are changed at regular intervals. This proves impractical for personnel who cover wide areas of the factory site.
   (c) Remote readers for card insertion are positioned at various access points and these are linked to a central computer control. This enables time zone and status level facilities to be incorporated and restricts the entry after working hours to authorized staff only. General movement and individual movement profiles can be made available.
   (d) Large companies issue all personnel with an identity card, including a photograph and this can be security coded to indicate approved access areas. Sophisticated systems would incorporate alarm systems to be put into action should unauthorized personnel try to gain access to a prohibited area.
2. The days of invisible ink have returned! A security marker is now available for the marking of one's own property. It can be used on most surfaces and the ink is invisible when dry. The writing reappears under ultra-violet light.
3. Many insurance companies require information on the security devices available on the premises when quoting for a policy to cover break-ins, damage, and theft.
4. In a small company it could be the responsibility of the secretary to keep abreast of deterrents and alarm systems. The British Security Industry Association and the National Supervisory Council for Intruder Alarms, as

well as trade pamphlets, will all help you to keep abreast of developments in this field.

5. Most modern computer systems have in-built security devices that prevent anyone who gains access to the computer being able to call up information. Special codes are built into the keying-in procedure and should be known only to the systems manager in charge of that particular program.

Short problems

You are secretary/receptionist in a professional office of architects in central London. Your offices are large and plush and the architects design mainly commercial property — offices including tower blocks, shops, and other facilities. The reception area is on the ground floor at the front of the building. You operate the small switchboard and look after the petty cash for incidental expenses working on an imprest of £50. Most clients are seen by appointment only.

How would you deal with the following situations?

1. A man in overalls calls to say he has come to service the central heating boiler which is in the basement. You are not aware that such a person is due to call.
2. It is near to Christmas and two nuns have called in collecting for the local children's home. They insist that companies in the vicinity have contributed not less than £5.

Suggested solution to problem 1
1. Ask to see his business card.
2. Ask him to take a seat in the lounge area which is out of earshot.
3. Ring through to maintenance to check if such a person was expected.
4. Check with the partners to see if such an arrangement had been made or with the landlord if the premises are rented.
5. Check that the company given on the business card exists in the telephone directory.
6. Verify with the company given on the business card that such a person is employed. (He may have been given the wrong address by his company.)

Assuming he is a bona fide employee and that the visit is genuine
7. Ask the man to sign the visitor's book.
8. Arrange for someone from maintenance to accompany him, particularly if there are any confidential documents stored in the basement.
9. Ensure that the man signs out when leaving.

Assuming he is a bogus employee
7. Telephone the senior partner and inform him of the steps you have taken and the discoveries made. He will probably elect to ring for the police.
8. It will be up to you to ensure that the man's suspicions are not aroused.

Suggested solution to problem 2
1. Establish which convent the nuns are from and then ask them to take a seat.
2. Check last year's petty cash book to see if a donation was made and how much.
3. You must decide whether giving donations of this kind are within your brief.
4. If in doubt verify with one of the partners.
5. If you are in any doubt as to the identity of the nuns, telephone their convent.

Assuming they are genuine
6. Give a donation, ignoring the 'sales patter' of £5, but ensure that a petty cash voucher has been signed by them.

Assuming they are bogus
7. Follow the same procedure as for the suggested solution to problem 1 under these circumstances.

Long problem
You work for the chief rating officer of your district council. It is Friday morning and he storms into the office with the local paper in his hand. He throws the paper onto your desk with the exclamation: 'Where the hell have they got the information from?' The headline that is disturbing him is shown below.

MASSIVE RATE INCREASES
Shock for Roydean residents

During the week you had prepared a table of the proposed rate increases which your boss and the borough treasurer had discussed *in camera.*

Immediately the phone rings and it is the borough treasurer's secretary asking that your boss be in his office at 1030 hours with an explanation.

How are you going to help your boss to investigate the security leak and what suggestions could you make to rectify this situation and prevent a repetition of such an occurrence?

Suggested approach

Before you start trying to discover how the information could have been obtained, read the article for yourself!

1. Are the figures quoted absolutely accurate?
2. Were the greatest increases for the Roydean area?
3. Could the headline be politically motivated — i.e., are council elections pending? Does Roydean have particularly active residents' associations?

Let us for the purpose of this problem make the following assumptions:

1. The figures quoted were generally accurate.
2. Roydean would in fact be faced with the greatest increase.
3. There would appear to be no political motivation.

The above assumptions would seem to confirm a security leak. How did the reporter get hold of these confidential figures? Was the reporter shown the figures or told about them?

Consider the ways the figures could have been seen in your office. Give this some thought, make a list, and check it with Fig. 10.1.

There is also the possibility that the document could have been seen in your boss's office.

Typing stage	- Office left unattended
	- A visitor to the office
	- Other members of staff
	- Discarded carbon ribbons
Spoilt copies	- Screwed up in the waste-paper basket
	- Torn up in the waste-paper basket
	- No shredder available
	- Left in the the bin after office hours
Photocopies	- Made by the technician
	- Not separated from non-confidential work
	- By other staff in the reprographics room
	- Original not removed from the bed of the photocopier
	- Check not kept on the number of copies dialled and printed
	- Machine fault with the copy left in the mechanism
Storage	- Copy left in the filing basket
	- Filing cabinet left unlocked
	- If on the word processor, storage disc left out
Mailing	- Sent to the mailroom or posted yourself?
	- Envelope not marked confidential

Figure 10.1   Ways in which the figures could have been seen in your office

Consider the ways in which the information could have been passed on by word-of-mouth. This is the human aspect of the problem and overlaps with confidentiality.

As we have assumed that the figures are accurate, the information could only have been disclosed by someone who had a good understanding of the situation as it is normally difficult to transmit statistics from memory. The information must therefore have come from you, your boss, or the borough treasurer.

With this in mind, consider how the information might have been imparted. See Fig. 10.2 when you have given some thought to the problem.

- Did you discuss the figures with your boss within earshot of anyone else?
- Could the intercom have been switched on during the discussion your boss had with the county treasurer?
- Was it mentioned on the telephone and could this indicate a leak through the switchboard?
- Was the discussion recorded in any way?

Figure 10.2   How the information could have been passed on by word of mouth

Now that we have identified how the information might have been leaked, how was it picked up?

1. Via a second person? (Probably a member of staff?)
2. Was an unauthorized person able to gain access? Does a check need to be made on reception security?

If this information was sent to the county treasurer's department, a security leak there cannot be discounted and would obviously require investigation. Rapid research would therefore be necessary before your boss's meeting with the county treasurer at 1030 hours.

To rectify the situation
1. How would you ensure that the outcry caused by the article was quelled as soon as possible?
   - Immediate contact with the paper.
   - Take the journalist involved to task.
   - Call a press conference.
2. How could the situation be explained to the council?
   - Prepare a report on investigations held and subsequent steps taken.
3. What steps would be taken to ensure that such a leak did not occur again?
   - There would obviously have to be a general tightening up on security

procedures. Consider also the commonsense precautions given in the introduction to this chapter.

One step further

How would you have dealt with the situation if:

- The figures had been only slightly accurate?
- The greatest rate increases did not apply to the Roydean area?
- A council by-election was pending?

Long problem

(**a**) Outline the problems which might arise from using the services of an outside computer and data processing bureau and indicate the safeguards that the client organisation should take in selecting and using such a service.

(**b**) What communication facilities might be used between the client organisation and the bureau and what considerations will govern the choice of the means of communication? (RSA PADip)

Suggested approach

If you are not sure of the services offered by a computer bureau, you should read the information about them in Unit 8. Our assumptions for answering this question are that you are using the facilities of the bureau as a batch user.

List the different sections of this question in order to help to organize your answer. You should have five subheadings:

1. Problems which might arise.
2. Safeguards in selecting.
3. Safeguards in using.
4. Communication facilities.
5. Considerations governing choice.

Problems that might arise

As a guide, there are three main areas in which problems might arise, viz:

Time factor   *Confidentiality and security*   *Errors*

Take each one separately and jot down your ideas on where you feel problems might arise. Check your ideas with those given in Fig. 10.3. Each point is coded either SS or SU indicating a Safeguard which could be taken when Selecting (SS) or Using (SU) such a bureau. Your next step should be to identify an appropriate safeguard for each point.

Time factor		*Code*
1. Data not ready on time.		SU
2. Creates a break in continuity for staff involved.		SU
3. Delivery delays upset bureau's scheduled workload.	SS	SU
4. Transportation and transmission of data.	SS	SU
5. Sudden appearance of urgent work.	SS	

Confidentiality and security		
6. Release of confidential information.	SS	SU
7. Objections by staff.	SS	
8. Disclosure of confidential information.	SS	
9. Loss of data *en route.*		SU

Errors		
10. Faulty media.		SU
11. Misinterpretation and misunderstanding of instructions and data.	SS	SU
12. Wrong data returned.		SU
13. Sequence of data wrongly presented.		SU
14. Under/over-charging.		SU

Figure 10.3 Problems that might arise in using a computer bureau

Obviously many of the problems you have identified could be avoided by careful selection at the outset.

Safeguards in selecting

For those problems identified and marked SS, give consideration to a safeguard you would take. You will find our safeguards given in Fig. 10.4.

3. Establish the flexibility of the agency with regard to agreed handover time and likely penalty if there is a deviation.
4. Establish times for receipt of data and also procedure for return of processed work.
5. Establish facilities for processing urgent work.
6. By ensuring that the bureau is a member of the British Computer Society you can
7. be confident that the staff will act discreetly in all matters of confidentiality and
8. this fact should be made quite clear to all your employees who are likely to have to use the services of this bureau.
11. Most bureaux disclaim responsibility for errors caused by poor quality of data at the time the contract is signed. However, before actually signing a contract it is advisable to have a sample batch processed in order to check on the efficiency, reliability, and quality of the work.

Figure 10.4 Safeguards when selecting a computer bureau

Safeguards in using
Repeat the process for those items marked SU. By now you should be more adept at identifying safeguards and this section should seem easier. Check with Fig. 10.5.

---

1. Ensure that strict time limits are set and adhered to for the production of data.
2. Re-education of staff to appreciate the merits of computer technology.
3. Keep bureau informed of any unavoidable delays.
4. Use of Datapost, Group 4, Securicor, or other specialists in the security field.
6. All data must be packed and sealed in special envelopes and consideration could even be given to the use of wax seals. Maintenance of a personal contact within the bureau itself would help to boost confidence in the safety of such data when out of the company's hands.
9. The use of a bona fide security company would reduce the risk of loss, but in any event a copy of all data should be kept on site.
10. Your employees must be made aware of the potential cost and delays that could occur as a result of faulty media being sent to the bureau.
11. A check should be made that the data to be processed are legible and that all instructions are clear.
12. If there is any likelihood that confusion could be caused by similarity of client names or work presented, a special code-name should be used. However, assurances should be sought from the bureau that full responsibility would be accepted by them should any mix-ups occur that are clearly their fault.
13. All documents or media should be safely packed so that the sequence cannot be lost if they are dropped or mislaid.
14. A procedure must be set up to record outgoing and incoming work. The record must indicate when work has been sent to the bureau and be put on permanent file.

Figure 10.5   Safeguards in using a computer bureau

Communication facilities
Most of the communication facilities have already been mentioned and you should now be able to list these without difficulty.

Considerations governing choice
1. You will see from the information given in Unit 8 that there are several types of bureau. Obviously a time-share contract could involve your company in considerable cost. On the other hand it would mean that no document would leave your premises.
2. A batch bureau would be cheaper and give greater flexibility but documents must go to the bureau to be processed.

3. Attention should be given to the time of day the batches of data are available and the fastest means of getting them to the bureau.

One step further
How would your investigations have differed had you been looking at using the time-sharing facilities of a bureau?

Additional problem
You are employed by a large ceramics company in the public relations department and you are responsible for organizing visits through the factory for groups of people from all walks of life. What steps would you take to ensure that security is maintained with regard to:

- Bomb scares?
- Industrial espionage?
- Pilfering?
- Vandalism?

11

The true meaning of secretary

But far more numerous was the herd of such who think too little and who talk too much.
DRYDEN (1631-1700)

Most jobs in the business world today involve the need for the maintenance of security and confidentiality to a greater or lesser degree. In secretarial work, however, it is of paramount importance. Indeed, as the word itself suggests, a secretary must be a person who is capable of keeping a secret.

Interpretation
We have just dealt with the more tangible aspects of this subject under *security*. There are, however, more amorphous areas — usually connected with human behaviour — when it is a little more difficult to define the term *confidentiality*.

The confidential environment
As a secretary your daily routine will not only include matters that are specifically confidential and recognized as such, but you will also live in a confidential environment. This means that you will hear and see a great deal that is not really meant for you:

- The telephone conversation when waiting for further dictation.
- Discussion taking place when serving coffee in the board room.
- The person being berated when you delivered the mail.
- The confidential document inadvertently left on a desk.
- The heated discussion you heard on the staircase.
- Your amazing ability to read upsidedown!

The information trap

These facts will invariably pass either into your subconscious mind and may never be recalled to the surface or, because of the stimulating nature of the information, they will immediately pass into your conscious mind and it is here that a quandary can arise:

1. Should you tell your friend this evening about the latest office gossip?
2. Would your friend like to know she's not getting a rise next week?
3. Should you tell his wife?
4. Does the information mean possible redundancy?
5. Could the information be used for commercial gain?
6. Isn't it nice to be the first to know?
7. Did anyone say to you 'Be discreet!'?

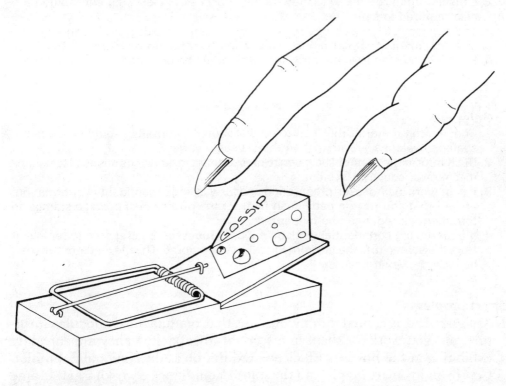

The information trap

Think First!

Whatever you may ultimately decide to do with the confidential information you have acquired, it is important that you should be able to go through a process of self-analysis in an attempt to justify your action:

1. Do you realize the importance of the information you have unwittingly gained?
2. Do you appreciate the full impact the divulgence of this information could have on the people concerned from a physical, mental, and emotional point of view. (Nervous breakdowns, ruined careers, and even bankruptcy have been caused by such disclosures.)
3. Would you in fact be betraying the trust placed in you?
4. In any event are you *sure* you heard or saw correctly?
5. And, if you pass this information on, is it likely to reflect back on you?

Do you know?

1. All civil servants have to sign an official secrets act declaration at least twice in their careers — when a job is taken up and when it is terminated.
2. Outside organizations who may be given access to classified information are also required to sign.
3. The civil service has a categorized system to identify the degree of confidentiality of a document ranging from top secret, confidential, to restricted.
4. People interested in joining the services should be prepared to undergo a strict screening procedure.

Snippets

1. Confidential material that has to be distributed internally should be placed in sealed envelopes — rather than the reusable variety.
2. Such information should be given to messengers to deliver as opposed to using a mechanical conveyor system.
3. If your work includes the preparation and forwarding of confidential information, ensure that you have a petty cash float for the purchase of postage stamps so that the mail room can be by-passed.
4. If undertaking confidential work on a word processor, be prepared to remove it from the screen into the file immediately if interrupted. The file medium can then be locked away if necessary.

Short problems

1. Modulec Ltd is a small family business that manufactures modular furniture and you work for them in a secretarial capacity. They are currently exhibiting at the Business Efficiency Exhibition at the National Exhibition Centre and you are helping on the stand. Your fiancé is working at the same exhibition on the Office Design Organization stand. This is a large company that specializes in office equipment and design as well as the type of furniture manufactured by your company. During the morning your representatives have had long discussions with buyers from a large multi-national organization and a substantial order is at stake. Over lunch your fiancé endeavours to find out from you the figures quoted. He works on a commis-

sion basis and such an order would make quite a difference to his income and his promotion prospects. How would you deal with this situation?

2. As a secretarial student you are doing a fortnight's work experience in a busy personnel department. It is the beginning of your second week and already you have undertaken a variety of duties that have helped to boost your confidence. The phone rings and, as the secretary with whom you are working is not in the office at the moment, you take the call. It is the production manager who wishes to check up on the personal details of one of his staff he is considering for promotion. As you know where the records are kept you give him the information. The secretary enters the room just as you are putting the phone down. She asks you who it was and you explain expecting praise for using your initiative. Her reaction is one of extreme annoyance. In what ways could she criticize your action?

Suggested solution to problem 1

1. As Modulec is small the loss of this order could jeopardize the future of the company.
2. First and foremost your loyalty should be with your company and not with your fiancé.
3. The loss of this order would have little effect on your fiancé's company because it is large and not solely reliant on the sale of this type of product.
4. You are employed in a responsible capacity and the company has faith in your integrity. Could you live with the knowledge that you had broken this faith?
5. It is also quite possible that the Office Design Organization will be able to quote lower prices in any case given their better production facilities.
6. The other side of the coin therefore is — if Office Design is also going to quote for this order, should *you* be pumping your fiancé for information?

Suggested solution to problem 2

1. Over the phone there is no way in which you could have obtained proof that the caller was, in fact, that person. It could have simply been a member of staff who was endeavouring to discover someone else's salary.
2. Even if you were sure that it was the production manager, this was a matter that should have been passed on to the secretary in charge.
3. Such information should not be given over the phone but sent under confidential cover.
4. As you were there for only a short time, you should not have been allowed access to the personnel records. By passing on this information you had undermined the secretary's confidence in you.
5. It would have been far better if you had explained to the manager that the

secretary was not there but that she would ring him back as soon as she came in. This would have verified the identity of the caller.

Case study

Instructions

Read the following case study very carefully. Analyse what you would have done under the circumstances. Turn to the flowchart which shows five possible routes with their appropriate outcomes (see Fig. 11.1).

Details

Sally Marsden works for the chief personnel officer (CPO) of a large manufacturing company with branches all over the country and abroad. She thoroughly enjoys her work which is varied and involves preliminary interviewing of junior staff and attending and taking the minutes of the management development committee (MDC) meetings, which discuss middle management progress within the company, and her boss reports directly to the board of directors on these meetings.

Sally is very friendly with another secretary, Jayne Phillips, who is three years younger than Sally and works for the assistant production manager, Adrian Bryant. Jayne also enjoys her work but finds her boss — a dynamic engineering graduate — rather abrasive and short-tempered towards her and other junior members of staff.

Over tea-break yesterday afternoon, Jayne confided to Sally that Adrian Bryant had applied for several posts outside the company within the last few weeks and that she hoped he would be successful as that nice Mr Mills was next in line for his job.

This was Sally's quandary

At the last MDC meeting, Adrian Bryant had been discussed and his future with the company had been outlined. He was proving to be extremely effective in his job and it was envisaged that within six months he would be ready to take over as production manager of the large Irish sister company when the current production manager was due to retire. Naturally such discussions are strictly confidential.

What should she do?

One step further

1. Would Sally have had the same problem if she had simply overheard that Adrian Bryant was applying for jobs?

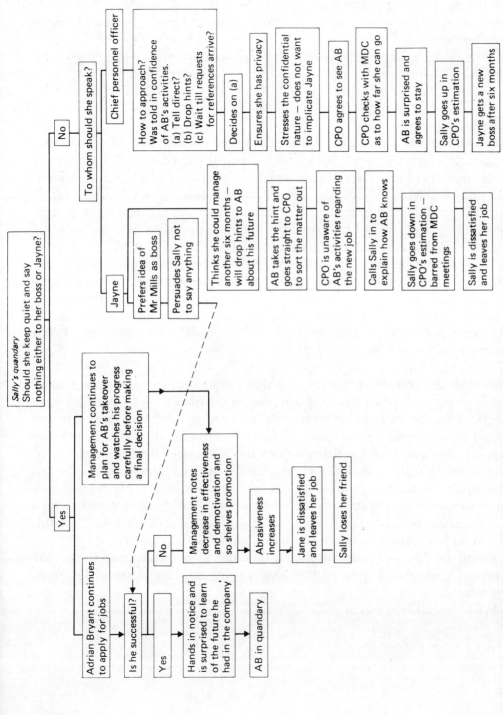

Figure 11.1 Flowchart showing five possible routes for Sally to take and their appropriate outcomes

2. Would Jayne's attitude have been different if she had got on well with Adrian Bryant as a person?

3. What might have been the outcome if Jayne had simply dropped hints to her employer?

4. List the points you have learned to take into consideration when presented with such a situation.

Additional problems

1. You work in the research and development department of a company producing cosmetics made solely from natural ingredients. This is a very competitive field and the research being undertaken is of a highly confidential nature. Every Thursday the results of analyses of your company's research products are produced by the computer and are handed to you for circulation to all the assistant research chemists prior to a meeting with the head of department that afternoon. For the past three Thursdays you have noticed that one of the assistants who has not been in your employ for very long has asked you for an outside line in order to make a phone call soon after you have distributed the figures. The normal procedure on phone calls is for you to make the call but on these occasions your offers to obtain the number have been refused, and this has aroused your suspicions. What action would you take and why?

2. Christine Myers works in a company that manufactures biscuits and cakes. She is secretary to the chairman and managing director and attends board meetings as the minute secretary. At a meeting held last Friday it was decided that consideration should be given to buying up a small company that is in the same field and apparently having financial difficulties. Christine knows that the father of a close friend is an area sales manager for this particular company and his area has just been extended. He is obviously unaware of the uncertain future of the company as he has decided to turn down another offer of employment with a well-known company because this would have meant a move to a different part of the country.

From the discussion at the board meeting it would appear that if the takeover goes ahead most of that company's employees would be made redundant.

What would you advise Christine to do?

Part Five

The personnel file

12

The personnel function

If I had a donkey wot wouldn't go,
d'ye think I'd wallop him? no, no, no.

BEULER (*Nineteenth century*)

'No man is an island' — this was written by John Donne in the fifteenth or sixteenth century and although the quote continues 'every man's death diminishes me because I am involved in Mankind' the quote *is* apt for the living because very few of us do live our entire private lives in solitude and, we would venture to say, that none of us can successfully exist in our working lives in complete isolation.

We all need to work *with* people and we all need to be *able* to work with people. In our social lives, we gravitate towards people with whom we share common interests, whose company we enjoy, and with whom we can be ourselves. In our business lives we have to make efforts to work with people with whom we may not have a natural affinity.

Today, employers recognize the importance of people in an organization and of providing pleasant working surroundings and conditions in which they can work efficiently. One of the functions of personnel departments in large companies is to try, by various means, to achieve harmonious working relationships.

Was it always so?

In bygone times, this was not always the case and people were exploited from a very early age. They worked to exist and some of them barely did that. There are plenty of industrial artifacts that bear witness to the way in which human beings spent their working lives. For example, the archaic equipment used in Cornish tin mines that exacerbated rather than prevented premature death from silicosis for a large number of people.

In 1819, the Factories Act was drawn up by Robert Owen. He himself had stopped employing children under 12 and provided better housing and recreation facilities for his workers.

Apart from the humanitarian aspect of his measures, he realized that a

139

better fed, more contented workforce worked harder, achieved better results, and profits increased.

The great industrial Quaker families also adopted a very humane approach to their workers and provided safe and clean working environments, more reasonable working hours, and better housing as well as elementary schools.

Thus, even as early as this, the importance of the well-being and morale of the workforce was recognized and these and many other considerations have led to the growth and increased specialization of the personnel function as it is today:

- The high cost of training and employing people.
- The importance of manpower planning.
- The complexities of the legislation affecting employees' jobs.
- The health and safety aspects of employing even a small number of people.
- The dire need to keep a contented, involved, and therefore productive workforce in the face of stiff competition.

First impressions
When applying for a job, your first personal contact with a large organization will be meeting and being interviewed by someone in the personnel department — an expert in interviewing people. You must, therefore, give some time and thought to how you are going to sell yourself.

You will probably have been given guidance and possibly attended mock interviews and you should, therefore, be aware of:

- The methods used to find out about you.
- The importance of preparation.
- The importance of having some knowledge of the particular business.
- The need to answer and to *ask* questions.
(Studying the job description should help you to formulate some questions.)

Have you, however, considered the first impression you will create? The unknown quantity is the rapport that may develop between you and the interviewer. A group interview, although initially offputting, can be beneficial in this respect — you have more chance of being drawn to one member of the panel. You should not, though, address her/him to the exclusion of the others.

At the end of the day, given three equally well-qualified people for a particular job, the deciding factor will be the personality of the applicant 'clicking' with that of the interviewer and the feeling that this person will fit into the existing team.

Looking after yourself

Once you have secured your job, your own particular needs may determine the satisfaction you achieve from it. If selection procedures are efficient, the job should be within your capabilities but is it challenging enough? If it is your first job, you may need time to settle down, to consolidate your skills, and to discover, if you can, in which direction this job will take you and if this is the direction in which you want to go.

If you are ambitious:

1. Can the job be a springboard to something higher either in this company or in another?
2. Can the job be expanded and your responsibilities increased as your capabilities and your knowledge of your boss and the company are extended?
3. Will further training in your own or in the firm's time extend your horizons?

Your performance appraisal interview, either official or semi-official, can increase your self-knowledge, by pointing out your strengths and weaknesses. It may even help you to capitalize on your strengths and minimize your weaknesses.

Looking after your staff

You may be responsible for junior members of staff. Are you able to deal effectively with them?

1. Can they approach you with their problems and do you listen to them?
2. Are you fair in the allocation of jobs or do you have favourites who get the most interesting ones?
3. When jobs are delegated do you constantly check up to see if the work is being done properly?
4. Have you any juniors who are frequently absent, late, moody, aggressive, or hostile?
5. Do you investigate the causes of any discontent?
   Was the induction course effective so that they know:
   - What to do?
   - Where to go?
   - What is expected of them?
   Are they being under-employed:
   - 'Sticking on stamps' or bored by 'endless filing' or 'typing technical tables that they don't understand?'
   Are they over-employed:
   - Constantly trying to beat the clock and never achieving it?
   - Overstretched — being asked to do jobs that are beyond them?

Are they insecure about:
- The machines they have to use?
- The lack of appreciation of their efforts?
- Their position in the firm — fear of redundancy?
- Their inability to communicate at all levels?

In your supervisory capacity you are responsible for managing a team — can you plan, organize, and coordinate the efforts of all concerned?

Do you consider their needs as well as the needs of the organization when setting up your work control plan?

Good relationships

Working for people, working with people, and having people working for you requires self-awareness, constant role adjustment, and effort in order to use the right approach to develop and maintain good personal relationships and enjoy the consequent harmony and satisfaction in your working life.

Everyone has off-days and the causes for this may be due to outside pressures or hurt feelings. Genuine attempts to understand may result in a greater awareness of people both at work and in your social life.

Thus, while the personnel department is responsible in broad terms for personnel morale, it is up to the individual employees to ensure that good relations are maintained in their particular sphere of contact.

Do you know?

1. How to write a good letter of application in order to sell yourself in your professional capacity without sounding too pompous?
2. What sections you would expect to find within a personnel department and what their functions would be?
3. What is the procedure from letter of application to appointment?
4. What to expect on your induction course?
5. Your legal rights as an employee?
6. The difference between a job specification, a personnel specification, and a job description?
7. What you would find in a contract of employment?
8. The meaning of 'bandwidth', 'core time', 'accounting period', and 'reconciliation' with regard to flexitime?

Snippets

1. The personnel manager has a functional relationship to all other line managers and is responsible for advising them on matters relating to staff.
2. Certain behaviour patterns may be indicative of low morale and dissatisfaction,

142

i.e., high rate of staff turnover, slipshod work, low output, frequent absences and unpunctuality, hostility, tense atmosphere, and even accidents.

3. A good supervisor should endeavour to foster a team spirit within her group but this is difficult if, among other things, working conditions are poor, there is no job security, the work is boring, and there are no prospects for promotion.

4. The 'grapevine' is a very real channel of communication in an organization but a strong, active grapevine indicates that formal channels are not efficient.

5. The seven-point plan was devised to help the interviewer to assess a candidate's suitability for a particular job and covers seven aspects — physical make-up, attainments, general intelligence, special aptitudes, interests, disposition; and circumstances.

Short problems

1. At your end-of-the-year performance appraisal your manager has pointed out the following weaknesses. What steps would you take to remedy these?
   (a) bad time-keeping,
   (b) nervousness in dealing with telephone enquiries,
   (c) difficulty in completing assignments on time,
   (d) inability to use the office junior's services to the best advantage. (LCC PSC)

2. For a boss/secretary relationship to be fulfilling and satisfying for both parties, it is essential that the boss must be able to delegate.
   What qualities would you, as a secretary, look for in your boss as a delegator?

Suggested solutions

1. (a) Bad time-keeping implies that it continues throughout the day — late arrivals and early departures.
   Late arrivals – morning
   Make sure you have a good watch, and that it keeps accurate time. If you are too rushed in the mornings and missing transport:
   - Decide on next day's clothes the night before.
   - Go to bed earlier during weekdays.
   - Rise earlier.
   - Investigate earlier transport.
   - Consider obtaining own transport.
   Late arrivals – lunchtimes
   Leave promptly for lunch. Calculate carefully the time needed for the journey back to work without rushing and the time needed in the cloakroom.
   Early departures
   No excuse. Leave at the stipulated time.

(b) Nervousness in dealing with telephone enquiries is possibly due to a lack of knowledge of the firm and its personnel.
- Try to be more knowledgeable about the firm and its products.
- Have a chart of the personnel in your department, the position held, and their extension number.
- Learn who deputizes for whom.
- Design a telephone message pad with possible courses of action listed if the person called is unavailable.
- Have you any phobias about using the telephone in business?
- Record yourself answering the telephone and be self-critical.
- Try to visualize the caller, smile with your voice, and remember that answering the telephone is an opportunity to project your company's image — use it!

(c) Difficulty in completing assignments on time may be due to working in a muddle and spending too much time in looking for papers. You may be starting too many jobs before finishing others.
- Reorganize your workstation and make use of baskets and pending files for work that cannot be finished for lack of information.
- Decide on your priorities at the beginning of the day, try to allocate time for each task, and maintain it. Collect any files and other information needed and any ancillary equipment.
- Keep interruptions to a minimum, such as chatting with other girls.
- If urgent tasks are presented to you, tidy away the task on which you are working and restart it immediately the urgent task is completed.
- Analyse your routine tasks and delegate where possible.
- Work methodically and in a calm frame of mind.

(d) Using junior's services can be encouraged by spending a short time each day to instruct her in routine jobs. When you are satisfied that she is able to cope you can delegate to her without over-supervising. Gradually increase the number of jobs for which she is responsible.
- After demonstrating any equipment, prepare instructions for her to follow herself without the need to keep bothering you.
- Teach her to use the filing system so that she can extract files and work with you on any big tasks given to you.
- Allow her to develop initiative without constantly breathing down her neck.
- Be approachable and make time to praise her if she deserves it.

Listed above are the practical steps that you could take to remedy weaknesses, but there may be underlying factors that are affecting your overall performance.

Bad time-keeping may be caused by lack of motivation — no responsibility, no interest, no prospects, no challenge — in fact, no job satisfaction.

Nervousness in dealing with telephone enquiries may be caused by insufficient opportunities to use the telephone, being unable to act as a filter or by being given an inefficient induction course that does not provide adequate background knowledge of the organization and personnel.

You may have difficulty in completing assignments on time because you may be over-worked or over-stretched and are asked to do jobs beyond the scope of the job description. The demoralizing effects would be reflected in bad time-keeping.

You may be unsure of the junior's role. Is a job description available? If you are over-worked, there may be no time to coach the junior. You may have a specialist job that does not warrant junior assistance. She may, therefore, be better re-deployed.

It is to be hoped that in the real situation, you would have discussed these and any other valid points during your performance appraisal interview.

Suggested solution to problem 2
Delegation is a two-way process and you must be capable of accepting delegated work just as much as your boss should be capable of delegating it.

How is delegation achieved?
Before handing over any work the boss must be able to plan ahead in order to determine his overall objectives and to decide how these will be achieved and who will be involved in specific tasks. He should identify responsibility areas and ensure that these are clearly delineated.

For delegation to be effective, he should be sensitive to people and capable of discerning how they should be treated. This understanding should ensure that he delegates tasks according to particular aptitudes and abilities and so helps to create and foster a team spirit.

Any manager must, however, ensure that he is impartial in his dealings with people and in the allocation of tasks; otherwise strong feelings of antagonism may ensue and cause a breakdown of the team.

Ideally, he needs to be approachable and willing to listen and to discuss any problems that may arise, thus remaining close to the workforce and not as a remote 'figurehead'.

He needs to be decisive and confident in his ideas but not so authoritarian that he is brusque or even threatening, which would probably result in little cooperation from all concerned.

It is, however, essential that he is able to communicate his instructions without fear of misunderstandings.

Ideally, if he is secure enough in his own position, he will allow you to develop and expand your job without the threat of losing power and control. This is one of the greatest causes of ineffective delegation throughout the whole of the organizational hierarchy and could equally apply to your feelings with regard to your junior.

Once you and your boss know the jobs to be delegated, this should increase your feelings of interest and involvement in the entire plan.

Case study

A year ago the Lambert Housing Group set up a central filing unit at their Lancashire headquarters. Sideways tracking systems were installed for the storage of paper documents.

Within the unit there is a microform section which is engaged in the rationalization of the system by converting paper files previously stored at the group's headquarters and branch offices into microform. It is also concerned with the immediate conversion of all drawings, plans, and maps into aperture cards, hard copies being forwarded as required to site managers. A retention policy has been instituted to control the amount of paper documents kept.

The control of the microforms is the responsibility of grade II filing clerks. On the other hand, grade I clerks, who tend to be employed straight from college, are engaged in the storage and retrieval of paper files. Requests are received via the automated internal mail system or by telephone, which is only answered by the central filing unit supervisor, who then completes a requisition slip.

General files are distributed through the internal mailing system but any confidential documents are retrieved and distributed personally by the grade II filing clerk with that additional responsibility.

Mrs Mavis Hanson is the supervisor in charge of the unit controlling the four grade II clerks in the microform section and the four grade I clerks in the paper storage and retrieval section. Of the four grade I clerks, three are permanently concerned with storage and retrieval and one maintains the out-system, tallying the requests for files with out-cards, preparing requests for return, plus carrying out such tasks as the preparation of new and replacing old or spoilt files.

Mrs Hanson has been in charge of the unit since it came into operation, during which time there has been a turnover of five grade II clerks and twelve grade I clerks.

The personnel manager has expressed grave concern about the situation and the expense and disruption involved, to the extent that the viability of the centralized unit is being questioned.

Mrs Hanson is also extremely worried, but all reasons given for leaving seem to have had little or nothing to do with the company. Mrs Hanson feels she has a good relationship with her staff. There have been no signs of overt rebellion against her personally or the methods she employs.

Today, Caroline Brown, a 17-year-old with a good educational background is leaving the unit because she has acquired a job in the marketing department that will enhance her career prospects. Caroline has been with the unit only three months. Mrs Hanson decides to talk with Caroline to see if she can throw any light on the situation.

Caroline is quite prepared to express her views in confidence.

These are the factors that she brings out as causes of the high rate of turnover:

1. Staff don't know what they are doing and how they fit into the organization. In fact they feel completely isolated.
2. They feel that they are treated like children.
3. There is a complete lack of continuity — the jobs they do don't lead anywhere.
4. They find the work boring and monotonous.
5. They feel it is a dead-end job with no prospects.
6. There is rigid control in a tense atmosphere.
7. They feel they are cooped up all day.

These revelations upset Mrs Hanson as it would appear that, if there is some truth in what Caroline has said, the finger of blame is pointing very firmly in her direction.

How would you help her to help herself and improve the situation in her department?

Suggested approach

What type of person is Mrs Hanson? Make your assumptions from the information given and list them before reading on.

1. Conscientious at work.
2. Not good with people — possibly her first supervisory job.
3. Concerned about the problems — apparently willing to listen and, if necessary, change.
4. Remote — unaware of staff needs.
5. Insensitive to the atmosphere.
6. Trying to maintain a tight, rigid system without explanations.
7. Unwilling to delegate.
8. Pleasant and harmless but lacking in strong personality.
9. Possibly insecure in her job. Afraid of losing control.

147

From the assumptions you have just made and the information given in the case study, identify the causes of the criticisms made by Caroline Brown. Consider each point made and list your ideas before checking with Fig. 12.1.

Consider the causes as shown in Fig. 12.1 and suggest ways in which this situation could be remedied so that staff would be encouraged to stay, be happy in their place of work, and thereby create stability and consequently improve efficiency. You will find considerable overlap in your suggestions. Our checklist is given in Fig. 12.2.

Factor 1	● Lack of induction course and lack of contact with other people creates a feeling of non-involvement and consequently no company loyalty.
	● Lack of structured training, particularly for grade I clerks, results in no specialization.
	● Lack of continuity in work means there is no follow through (an unavoidable result of centralization).
Factor 2	● Rigid control.
	● Lack of delegation — not even answering the phone.
	● For grade I clerks, the status division between them and the more senior grade II clerks increases their feeling of inferiority.
Factor 3	● No job satisfaction.
	● No responsibility.
	● Caused by points raised under factor 1.
Factor 4	● All staff kept to one particular job.
	● No variety of work during the day.
Factor 5	● No extension of capabilities either within the unit or outside.
	● No self-fulfilment or sense of achievement.
	● No motivation.
	● No apparent opportunities for further study.
	● No apparent career structure for junior clerks.
Factor 6	● No opportunity to use initiative — over-organization leads to working in isolation and therefore no team spirit.
Factor 7	● Only one person allowed out.

Figure 12.1   The causes of the criticisms made by Caroline Brown

- Introduction of, or improvement in, an induction course.
- Noticeboard — increase awareness of sports and social events.
- House magazine — keep staff informed of developments.
- Training on machinery.
- Clear explanation of systems when staff join the unit.
- Opportunities for day-release.
- Career-structured training programme — rotation of staff between centralized services — providing better career prospects.
- Better selection methods for increased compatibility of staff.
- Increased delegation/trust/responsibility.
- Delegate responsibility for answering the phone.
- Treat all staff equally — no favourites.
- Suggestions box to improve the systems.
- Encouragement of cooperation between staff.
- Frequent meetings to discuss problems/changes.
- Closer liaison with staff — should be more approachable.
- Rotation of jobs — opportunity for younger ones to change.
- Rota for delivery of confidential files.
- Encouragement of happy atmosphere — posters/plants/radio, if allowed by management.
- Frequent breaks to alleviate monotony.
- Improved environment.
- Bonus/incentive scheme.

Figure 12.2   Checklist of changes to be made in order to improve staff relations

One step further
Draw up:

1. A suitable induction course for employees about to take up work in centralized service departments.
2. A careers development programme for college leavers to train and work in the centralized service units of: filing reprographics, mail, and audio/word processing.

Long problem
Starrad is a manufacturing firm of central heating radiators and boilers. Its main plant is on a widespread site and incorporates the administration, as well as the manufacturing, side of the business.

Production workers commence work at 7.45 a.m. and finish at 4.15 p.m. — lunch break is between 12 and 12.45 p.m. with a 10-minute break in the mornings at 10.30 and in the afternoons at 2.15. Office staff on the other hand work from 9 to 5.15 with lunch from 12.45 to 1.30 and breaks at 11 a.m. and 3 p.m. There are canteen facilities for all staff providing substantial, subsidized meals. All drinks are obtained from vending machines in strategically placed break-areas throughout the plant.

For many years on-site dental and chiropody treatment has been available for all employees. The board of directors has now decided, however, that these services must be discontinued because of the increasing costs of maintaining them.

The various trade union representatives are opposed to this decision for several reasons among which are the possibility of loss of earnings as well as the inconvenience that will be caused both to the employees and to the company through personnel having to make appointments during working hours.

The possibility of introducing flexitime has been raised in the past and the board now feels that perhaps the time is right to introduce such a system in view of the recent decision to discontinue the dental and chiropody service. They have therefore — somewhat belatedly — set up a working party to represent all interested parties and you are a member of this team.

The aims of the party are as follows:

1. To investigate the feasibility of introducing flexible working hours for all employees of the company.
2. To identify those areas where such an introduction would prove impractical.
3. To suggest how this might effectively be put into operation for those sectors where the introduction would be practicable.
4. To investigate and identify the equipment needed to run and monitor such a system.
5. To suggest a means of gauging employee support for this system.

You may make any further assumptions you feel necessary but they should be clearly stated. If possible, you should work with two or three colleagues and, after investigations, draw up a formal report showing your findings, conclusions, and recommendations.

Suggested approach

Assumption areas
1. Decide on the position of the plant (in town/out of town) and the availability of public transport (or the need for special transport facilities).
2. The situation regarding over-time — if worked and by whom.
3. Decide on an organization chart including ancillary services such as cleaning and gardening.

4. Is there a security control and is the plant either open or watched 24 hours a day?

5. Has the company its own transport system for making deliveries? What is the pattern for incoming goods — e.g. mainly on Monday, Wednesday, and Friday mornings?

6. Are goods produced using a straight production line or has the company a system of quality circles?

7. What is the total number and distribution of personnel?

8. Is there any mechanized time-keeping equipment or systems already on site?

9. Decide on the current level allowed for authorized absences with pay.

Identify clearly the present situation

1. Total the number of hours worked per week per man by production and office staff.

2. How many hours do you feel may, on average, be lost per person by:
- Dental/chiropody appointments?
- Authorized absences (hospital appointment, etc.)?

Identify those sectors of workers who, by virtue of their jobs, could not work flexihours
A great deal will depend here on the additional assumptions made. Would you recommend any extra concessions for these workers?

Identify those sectors of workers for whom flexitime would be feasible

1. Need to differentiate between manufacturing and administration?

2. What factors will limit flexibility of flexihours?

3. Investigate recording and monitoring equipment available.

4. Obtain leaflets and identify difficulties or drawbacks.

Gather your conclusions and set out appropriately

Work out a flexible system of working for all employees concerned

1. Apply the pre-set parameters on which the principles of flexitime are based.

2. Where possible, show your recommendations in graphic form.

Identify any subsequent effects this is likely to have

1. On requests for time off.

2. On holidays.

3. On working routine.

Put forward your recommendations for a back-up system
1. Wages and salaries computation.
2. Staff information service.
3. Staff feedback system — at least for the first few months.

One step further
Design a questionnaire to find out the employees' reactions to the system, which has been in operation for some two months.

Part Six

What of the future?

13

People or machines?

An expert is one who knows more and more about less and less.
BUTLER (1862-1947)

The technological boom over the last few years caused by the advent of the silicon chip has been termed by some a 'revolution' and by others an 'evolution'. Whatever the term used, there is little doubt that its development has had a dramatic effect on office life and no one knows where it will end.

A similar change was wrought when the transistor was developed and computers of a manageable size became feasible. At that time the general feeling was that this heralded the end of industry's need for manpower. Instead it created a whole new range of jobs that had never previously been thought of.

At the moment the problem is that no one can as yet foresee the full impact of these developments in terms of the re-deployment of manpower. It is difficult to forecast what the new spin-off jobs to emerge from this revolution will be, and it is perhaps this uncertainty that is causing the modern-day Luddites to get to work to increase the fear and hence the antagonism towards these huge technological advances.

To some extent the microprocessor has brought a mini-boom to industry in otherwise difficult times — the enormous increase in the number of electronic games, calculators, washing machines, ovens, music centres, telephones, pagers, audio systems, etc., are all being marketed on those magic words 'microprocessor technology' and are achieving great success.

The word processing/microcomputer craze (and the word is used advisedly) has even had its effects on the office furniture industry. This field had remained relatively stable for many years. Now it is developing rapidly with fully-adjustable, cable-ducted workstations, new style chairs, anti-glare finishes, and pedestals that tilt, tip, and turn.

Researchers are also trying to find the snags attached to the new technology. One of the main areas of contention is with those engaged in screen-based work. Information on this subject is given in Unit 3.

However, is society (and the business executive in particular) educated to accept, understand, use, appreciate, and recognize the pitfalls of this new technology?

Small is beautiful

Companies may be getting larger and larger but chip-controlled equipment is getting smaller and smaller. The capability to build in so much logic into a space the size of a pinhead is resulting in increased flexibility, capability, and overlap of equipment. Previously the function of one piece of equipment was clearly defined — a photocopier was a photocopier and nothing else; a switchboard was a control centre for telephone calls and nothing else — computers and automatic typewriters were completely separate.

Now the job barriers are down, 'systems', 'networks', and 'stations' are definitely 'in', and the black/white distinction is getting decidedly grey.

This development can clearly be seen in the word processor/microcomputer field.

Dedicated word processors were thought to be essential if correspondence quality was to be achieved, and the machines were to be 'user friendly'. Computer software conversion packages were complicated and limited in their scope. Conversion packages have now been developed that make multifunction computers completely viable in the word processing field. By the same token, word processors are taking on more and more data processing functions — notably, maths, sort, and graphics. Thus the difference between the two grows less and less, the result being an 'information centre'.

Machines were to be 'user-friendly'

The photocopier in the modern world

'Smart' copiers offer a wide range of functions and are no longer the straight-forward copier that has been around in offices for many years and that will, no doubt, continue to be there for some time.

1. Selection of type styles and sizes and paper orientation is computer controlled.
2. Laser character generation onto paper may be from a digital source (such as a word processor/computer terminal/host computer) — a 'master' is no longer essential.
3. Forms, charts, logos, and even signatures are stored electronically and can be re-created upon demand using laser technology. This eliminates the need for a store of standard pre-printed forms. Also it ensures perfect placement of information on the form. There are no poor carbons — each is an original.
4. Automatic distribution of information between copiers and through network systems to workstations is possible. The smart copier is thought by some to be the future replacement for fax.
5. Buffer function queues jobs while the system is in operation.
6. Combined with a phototypesetter and a laser platemaker (for offset litho machines which are now also microprocessor-controlled and the only office-based source of fully coloured artwork) a complete print centre is provided.

Telephonic links

These fall into two basic categories: internal and external.

Internal

Decentralized systems are possible by installing an infinitely expandable number of individually controlled microprocessor-based units that combine intercom/internal phone and paging functions and can be plugged in anywhere using a standard electrical point.

The facilities they offer are numerous:

- Conference calls.
- Hurry-up tone to indicate to a busy line that a call is waiting.
- Automatic busy station call-back (avoids constant dialling of busy numbers).
- Priority facility to enable calls to be interrupted.
- Remote control — doors, conveyors, lighting systems — can be operated.
- Automatic redirection of calls — caller is unaware of redirection.
- Block to prevent incoming calls when the user does not wish to be disturbed.
- Two-way mobile radio facilities.

- Digital display to see which extension is calling.
- Link to paging system.

External

External calls may be controlled and monitored by a central computerized PABX (or EDX — electronic digital exchange) which is capable of much more than accepting and processing incoming and outgoing calls, for instance:

- Simultaneous transmission of data, fax, and speech through the same system.
- Abbreviated dialling codes for speedier access to regularly used numbers.
- Conference facilities.
- Accounting control of calls.
- Logging and analysis of calls.
- Priority on outgoing calls for predetermined executives.
- Varying facilities for staff according to their needs.
- Access to calls can be restricted during busy or high tariff periods.
- Flexible enough to enable an otherwise restricted number to make calls when needed.
- Costs outgoing calls which are displayed on a meter.
- Access to central dictation unit transferring all commands to the user once contact has been made.

Electronic mail

There appears to be two basic interpretations of what constitutes an electronic mailing system:

Electronification of standard mailroom equipment

- Scales that give correct postage are read out. (Replaceable chip as postal rates change.)
- Linked to franking machine that automatically sets to correct amount.
- Electronic metering of mail to give debit/credit balance by department.
- Mail processors that moisten, seal, and frank.
- Mailing of computer output: separates, folds, inserts, seals, and franks.
- Automatic classification to ensure optimum postal rebates.
- Addressing machines with dual disc drive together with an automatic labeller. Random access memory allows incorporation of selection codes giving random access to addresses according to classification. Uses bi-directional dot matrix printer.
- Bomb detectors — X-ray scanning devices.

158

Distribution of 'mail' in digital form
This gives greater speed and accuracy, eliminates loss and delay, and promotes speedier decision-making.

'Mail box' computer
Data are posted and stored electronically. Computer access is via specially interfaced terminals (portable or fixed).

What happens?

- User logs onto the computer using his own identification and password either to access his own mail box or to enter data for transmission. It may be used for intra-company correspondence or by travelling/remote users.
- Messages only go to the central processing unit (CPU) and can be retrieved by users from any terminal.
- A document can be given a priority rating.
- When accessing the mail box, a list of messages waiting can be called to screen.
- 'Reply requested' code can also be incorporated ensuring reply before other mail is dealt with.
- It provides 24-hour links.

Communicating word processors
Automatic transmission may be made between compatible machines from screen to screen using telephone lines.

Speedier telex
- Electronic telex machines combine an off-line creation on screen with a simultaneous transmission of previously prepared material.
- Telex management systems enable the creation of material on a variety of terminals with access to the system.

What happens?

- The telex number and answer-back code is inputted followed by the message. The management system then takes over and automatically dials, retries, and transmits messages.
- It provides confirmation of transmission to the originator.
- It allows simultaneous acceptance of incoming messages and distribution of them to the screen.
- It gives multiple destination distribution, priority routing, and call accounting.

Facsimile transceivers
- It is possible to transmit a pre-loaded batch of documents.
- Light emitting diode (LED) or liquid crystal display (LCD) show time and date plus the connecting number are provided.
- A key pad enables input of security codes to prevent access by unauthorized personnel.
- All incoming documents are automatically printed with time and date.
- Faster transmission is achieved by a white line skipping facility.

Electronic filing

While the office of the future may not be completely paperless, a great deal of information will not only be distributed in digital form, it will also be stored in this way as well as in microform and as paper in the traditional way.

What happens?

- From paper using smart micro-image terminal, the document is converted into microform which in turn is filed electronically.
- Documents are re-called by keying in the appropriate code-name or number and the document then appears on a local or remote screen in microform or can be brought out as hard copy.

Total communications networks

The ultimate in the electronic office is an interlinked system of terminals, local and remote workstations, and dedicated function, shared, host computers. Communications links can also be interfaced to give compatibility between the system and other equipment or similar but separate systems, thus giving the prospect of an infinite communications network.

What happens?

- Work may be originated at a secretarial workstation on a screen.
- The document is committed to file, i.e. it is stored in the dedicated function shared resources computer, which operates as a replica manual filing system using the codes of 'drawers', 'folders', and 'documents'. This analogy makes the system more 'user friendly'.
- Because this unit also acts as the electronic 'mail centre', this document could be 'filed' in the addressee's 'mail box' to await his attention. Should the document be intended for distribution, the inputting of a mailing list would ensure that the requisite number of 'copies' were prepared and delivered to the mail boxes as required.

- The executive too operates a workstation — by a screen and remote touch sensor. On the screen, pictorial representations of such items as file baskets, folders, drawers, etc., appear — the remote touch sensor enables these to be located by the cursor which activates that particular function. Basic editing facilities are also available.
- If hard copies are required, the print-dedicated computer is contacted and hard copies are produced using laser generation with flexibility of type style and sizes.

Thus, with such a system operating on an intra-company basis documents can be passed throughout the company in electronic form.

Electronic typewriters

It is felt that these are likely to become the secretary's standard tool. Most secretaries doing non-routine work do not need the wide and sophisticated capabilities of a word processor, yet several word processing functions are extremely useful for any sort of work, i.e.:

Emboldening	*Automatic carriage return*
Decimal tabs	*Automatic centring*
Multi-pitch	*Automatic correction*
Any key repeat	*Automatic inset*
	Automatic right hand margin justification
	Automatic underscore

plus a limited character memory.

These features are available in a wide range of electronically operated typewriters. Some have a standard type keyboard while others have a flat touch sensitive 'key' board.

The cost of electronic typewriters is on the decrease and so companies will not baulk at replacing the old, obsolete manual and electric models. To some extent the change will be forced upon them by the fact that major typewriter producers are eliminating or cutting back on the production of traditional models.

When is an electronic typewriter not a word processor?

Machines with under 2K permanent memory are considered to remain as typewriters while those with more than this memory capacity come into the realms of word processors. Additionally, a dividing line is made between those machines that operate intelligently and those that do not. Except for a small line screen, which is available on some models of electronic typewriters, they do not have a screen as do word processors.

Screen orientated versus paper orientated

It must always be remembered that no matter what a particular machine may be capable of doing, man was at the root of the creation of that capability. There is and always will be room for original thought. Nevertheless, if we are to fit in with the new technological society, attitudes must change. We live in what is still primarily a paper-based society. Our mental reaction to the word 'book' is that of a neatly bound pile of papers. Similarly, when we are working it is normal to use a piece of paper for our jottings. This attitude must in large part change, if the technological advances are to be taken to their ultimate conclusion with a resultant enormous saving on world resources. Society must become screen-orientated, i.e., be prepared at any time (not just at work) to input onto a screen, edit on a screen, and read from a screen. Eventually, even bed-time reading could be done in this way! Nevertheless it is a serious attitude of mind that must permeate through, not only to the clerks and secretaries but also to the echelons of management if the information network systems currently available are to be successful.

The future now

How is this transition to be achieved? Is it to be slow and gradual or must it come in an organized fashion with meaningful dialogue between management and men to allay fears and disquiet among the workforce and to plan for the equipment's total integration into the organization? Our teaching establishments must surely take the lead in preparing students to acquire the necessary attitudes and skills to fit into the office of the future.

Do you know?

1. If you had to select a word processor, what operations you would expect it to be able to undertake?
2. The meaning of facsimile telegraphy, how it works, and its advantages?
3. The different types of pager available, their limitations, and how, in high-noise areas, a holder can be informed that contact should be made?
4. The use — even in this high technology era — that can be made of control boards for staff location, production, deployment of staff and machines, staff training, shift rotas, maintenance planning, and even computer loading?
5. That audio machines are now electronically controlled and have LED display to indicate the number and ends of letters, together with special instruction indicators. There is also a flashing cursor to indicate the position on the tape

162

and an automatic pause and warning note at the beginning of each piece. Some machines have a second track for 'afterthoughts' to allow the insertion of additional or changed material at appropriate points — the typist is warned when an afterthought feature has to be used by a tone on the tape.

6. That centralized dictation management systems automatically switch a dictator to the typist who can deal with his work the soonest, by comparing work left to be done with typists' speeds. Others have visual display units (VDUs) for supervisory use, which give up-to-date information on throughput of work.

Snippets

1. Updatable, replaceable, and deletable microfiche are available, produced on a photoplastic film by an electrostatic process and heat.
2. A telex pad is available that allows handwritten creation of telexes for direct conversion into electronic form for transmission.
3. Computer-aided design (CAD) and Computer-aided manufacturing (CAM) terminals are available that are programed to aid design engineers to calculate such things as stress, tolerances, quantities and types of material, and adherence to safety standards and to accept free-hand drawings.
4. Teleconferencing that is currently available will be improved with the addition of an 'electronic blackboard' to enable those involved to see the document or article under discussion.
5. For the person on the move there is a mini word processor. It only has 5 keys on the main keyboard, a 12-character moving display, and a 6 A4-page memory. Input is by simply keying into the system It can be connected to a TV set with an adaptor. Sixteen lines of text can be called up at once for editing on the screen or for printing. It is useful for meetings and speeches. There are devices to adapt its use for the blind and deaf. It can be used by outworkers attached to word processing agencies.
6. Closed circuit television (CCTV) is being used to access paper documents in centralized filing systems. It has conference facilities and the added attraction that papers do not leave the filing unit.
7. A portable microfiche reader is available which is battery operated or can be plugged into the car cigarette lighter.
8. **For the disabled:**
    - Several electric typewriters are available with guards and shields to enable those with finger tremor to type.
    - Office electric typewriters can be converted for those with no hand movement, using the suck and blow principle. They can also be adapted in other ways so that very heavily handicapped people can use them — even by using the eyelids.
    - IBM have developed an 'audio-typing unit', which is in effect a voice synthesizer that can be used with any IBM memory typewriter and gives voice playback by letter or word (with unlimited vocabulary). It should be of great use to blind typists who usually have to rely on the sighted for assistance when proof-reading.
9. Some word processors print out edited areas in red on the first post-adjustment printout to aid proof-reading.
10. For the poor speller some machines have a 250 000 word spelling verification dictionary.

11. Collators on photocopiers have been with us for some time but now it is also possible for the completed sets to be jogged and stapled — automatically!
12. Speech recognition systems are available in which the voice is converted to a digital representation in order to build up a reference template — each user having his own. The spoken code-word activates the search-and-find facility and recalls the information to the screen. It is useful in 'hands occupied' situations, for handicapped people, and in the sterile situation.
13. Various callmakers enable calls to be stored in a memory, thus allowing single number calls to be made or automatic dialling of the last number dialled manually.
14. Pagers may be the responsibility of the receptionist for collection when personnel are leaving the premises. It may also be her responsibility to ensure that they are put in the recharging unit.

Short problems

1. The technological boom brought about by the development of the microchip has brought with it new terminology. What are the meanings of the following commonly used words and phrases?

Smart	User friendly	Shared resource
Remote	Interface	Dedicated
Digital	LED	Correspondence quality
Intra-company	Inter-company	

2. Assuming that you have a good range of up-to-date equipment at your disposal, how would you:
   (a) Get an important letter received in the mail this morning to your boss who is currently in New York? An immediate answer is required to this letter.
   (b) Contact the maintenance man who is working on top of the roof of one of the production sheds?
   (c) Know that the phone in your office was not ringing endlessly while you worked with a colleague in his office?
   (d) Gather an *ad hoc* committee's findings together when members are spread over a large industrial site, and prepare a report for consideration at the next meeting?
   (e) Operate a microcomputer when working in the laboratory and wearing the statutory protective clothing, including rubber gloves?
3. You work for a small-businessman whose business is rapidly expanding. You are increasingly finding yourself involved in envelope typing both to clients and suppliers. You are concerned that this invariably means a backlog of other work and to you this tedious task seems an awful waste of time. Your boss has said he will consider any equipment you feel would help you in this task but would prefer to avoid a large capital outlay. What would you suggest?

Suggested solution to problem 1

1. *Smart* is an American term which in the UK is often substituted by *intelligent*. This means that the equipment in question has a decision-making capacity built into it and is capable of making decisions given the necessary parameters.

2. *User friendly* — in order to make equipment more acceptable to the general office worker as opposed to the technically-orientated buff, manufacturers have endeavoured to design machines that operate on easily understood commands using normal basic English. In this way the functions of the machines are much more easily understood and the amount of antagonism towards them is reduced.

3. *Shared resource* — a computer that is capable of serving more than one terminal or word processor.

4. *Remote* — as you would expect from the meaning of the word, a terminal or access point that is some distance away from the centre of the action whether it be a telex, computer, microform reader, etc.

5. *Interface* — an electronic means of connecting two dissimilar pieces of equipment together to make them compatible.

6. *Dedicated* — equipment that is designed, programmed, and used for a single function only.

7. *Digital* — in order that documents can be understood by a computer they must be converted into a mathematical language. This form is often referred to as 'digital' and is the way in which documents are inputted, stored, and retrieved by the computer.

8. *LED* — light emitting diode — a series of diodes that, when current is passed through them, light up in the appropriate shape of the letter or figure keyed in — most commonly seen on calculator read-out screens.

9. *Correspondence quality* — refers to printers and the quality of the print they produce. Dot matrix printers are generally considered unsuitable for correspondence though developments are taking place by which the number of dots is being increased to give a more acceptable quality.

10. *Intra-company* — within the same company.

11. *Inter-company* — between different companies.

Suggested solution to problem 2

(a) Fax would seem to be the most appropriate method to use here. Transmission is quick and easy and fax machines can receive information 24 hours a day, thus overcoming the time difference. Your boss would also be able to make any appropriate notes on the transmitted document and transmit it back to you. With careful timing, this can be done within a working day between UK and the States.

(b) The employees in the maintenance department should be issued with pagers so that they can be contacted — most important as they may be needed urgently. Similarly, when doing jobs in awkward places, contact with fellow employees could save time if extra equipment or tools were needed. A radio pager would be more appropriate in this instance so that a two-way conversation could take place and an estimate as to the urgency of the job you need doing could be given without his having to get to a phone. If, because he is working on the roof of a production shed, noise is a problem, the pager could be fitted with a beamed light to indicate that contact should be made. In order for you to be able to contact this person you would need an intercom with a radio paging facility. Alternatively, a bleeped 'code' could be used to indicate to the maintenance employee what he should do.

(c) With a microprocessor-controlled internal system and a computerized PABX all calls could be coded to be diverted automatically to your temporary number.

(d) Individual members could have their findings keyed in at secretarial workstations at their own remote points and this information could be mailed electronically to your own mail box. All this could then be called to a screen at your own station, edited, and formatted to your requirements. Once you had achieved the results you required, the report could be dispatched in digital form to the smart copier where, for the first time, a hard copy would be produced.

(e) The problem here is that the hands are being used and it could be dangerous to remove protective gloves in order to operate the keyboard. Therefore some other means of activating the keyboard would seem desirable. There are two ways in which this could be done:
- Using a speech recognition terminal, information could be recalled to screen by saying the appropriate code words but this would necessitate the wearing of a microphone.
- Touch terminals are available that have a screen showing a number of user-programmable 'touch points' with a menu of options displayed on the screen. The user need only touch the appropriate point to activate the machine.

Suggested solution to problem 3
There are various methods available:

Hand-addressing machine   It is cheap but messy and relatively slow. You would still be occupied.

Automatic-addressing machine   This is a faster machine but involves huge capital investment and amortization would therefore take a long time. The volume would probably not warrant the purchase. It is a single-function machine.

Electronic typewriter Memory capacity would soon be exhausted as it is difficult to retain permanently if the memory is used for other purposes. A typewriter like this would be an additional useful asset (assuming you only have a standard electric or manual model).

Word processor It is a huge capital outlay, although leasing can be considered. An addressing program is possible but it would have to be supervised to ensure good registration onto the envelopes or labels. Other uses for the machine would have to be identified to warrant the purchase. It has the capacity for random selection if so programmed.

Photocopier Desk-top models are available at reasonable lease rates with immediate repairs service. Adhesive labels can be used on it and master sheets ensure perfect registration. It cuts the preparation time down. The copier would perhaps be more appropriate for a small business because of its multi-purpose uses. It involves low capital outlay for relatively sophisticated equipment. Random selection, however, would be difficult.

Case study
Six months ago, Julie Field took up a post as assistant training officer with the Nettlewick Corporation, which has re-sited its headquarters and manufacturing plant in her area.

Initially she was involved in organizing seminars for middle and top management to enable them to become familiar with the new electronic office systems that had been installed.

She is now involved with the organization of the induction courses for trainee managers and other replacement management staff. At the last board meeting it was decided that these courses should be restructured to include a familiarization programme on the resources available so that new recruits will understand them and be ready to use them in the future.

Equipment to be included in the courses
- Information processing centre including word processors and the centralized dictation unit.
- Telex management system.
- Computerized PABX and decentralized internal system.
- Facsimile transceivers.
- Mainframe computer and departmental terminals.
- Centralized filing unit with microform and paper storage.

How, if you were Julie, would you organize the induction course to meet the requirements of the board?

Suggested approach

Before you begin to plan an induction course you need to ask and answer a number of questions:

1. What do the new employees need to know in general:
    (a) About the company?
    (b) About the personnel?
    (c) About the job itself?
    (d) About facilities and benefits?
    (e) About safety and security?
    Our suggested list appears in Fig. 13.1.

(a) *About the company*
- Tour of the company (factory and offices) to find their way around.
- Background history, current position, and future plans of the company to appreciate the standing of the company.
- Organization chart to understand the company's hierarchy and the horizontal and vertical integration pattern.

(b) *About the personnel*
- Organization chart — to see the titles of key personnel.
- Meet key personnel — heads of department, section leaders.
- Meet the people in the department where they will be working first of all.
- Meet trade union representatives.

(c) *About the job itself*
- Terms and conditions of employment.
- Job description.
- First month's programme.
- Union membership.

(d) *About facilities and benefits*
- Welfare.
- Fringe benefits.
- Sports and social club.
- Canteens.
- Training programmes.

(e) *About safety and security*
- Meet safety representative — accidents and safety procedures.
- Production of identity card.
- Allocation of security access card.
- Car park — zone allocation, identification disc, registration number of car to records.

Figure 13.1   Checklist of information about the company that new employees would need

2. How would you achieve the aims of the board with regard to the familiarization programme on the available resources?

You need to bear in mind the validity of explanations, demonstrations, practice, and written information when incorporating each item of equipment in your course.

Our suggestions on how we would introduce the equipment to the trainee managers are shown in Fig. 13.2.

Word processors	Skilled operator (possibly a senior secretary or supervisor) to demonstrate their functions and explain applications for managers; identify scope of usefulness.
Telex	Explanation and demonstration of off-line creation and automatic transmission given by the communications room supervisor.
Internal and external phones	Facilities explained with a practical session including guide to usage, security control, and the call accounting system.
Centralised filing unit (CFU)	Visit to CFU — demonstration of the creation and retrieval systems and the operation of remote terminals — practical session.
Fax	Explanation of uses and demonstration of the method of operation.
Dictation unit	Information on command codes, see unit in operation, meet staff in the unit — 'personalizes' future contact, operate system.
Mainframe computer	Demonstration of loading, uses, and terminal access given by the chief systems engineer.

Figure 13.2   Checklist on how to introduce the available equipment to trainee managers

3. How much time is likely to be needed?

You have now got a list of those items — technical and non-technical — that should be covered in the induction course for trainee managers. Go through the list and allocate an appropriate amount of time for each item. Do not separate those items that should logically be grouped together. Do not be surprised if you need to spread the course out over several days.

Designing the course
The actual placing of items on the course would in reality depend to a large extent on the availability of staff. Nevertheless, certain guidelines need to be adhered to:

1. Give a good welcome and encourage a sense of belonging from the start.
2. Let new staff find their whereabouts as soon as possible.
3. Do not 'blind with science' by showing too much equipment at once.
4. Allow time for questions and any personal difficulties.
5. Any 'handouts' or information sheets should be neatly presented in a folder so that they are retained and not simply 'lost'. This is very important if instructions for use are given.

Following these guidelines, incorporate all the topics in a course, together with times and any other details you wish to include.

One step further
Devise a short re-training programme for executives who will be required to operate an executive workstation as part of the electronic mailing system.

14

Where do I go from here?

'Are you not', a Rugby master had asked him in discussing one of his (schoolboy) essays, 'a little out of your depth here?' 'Perhaps, Sir,' was the confident reply, 'but I can swim'.

IREMONGER ON ARCHBISHOP WILLIAM TEMPLE (1881-1944)

'Everyone lives by selling something' (R. L. Stevenson 1850-1894) and we believe that from the moment we embark upon working for qualifications to enable us to do a specific job, we are thinking of selling our services and our talents to earn a living either by being employed or by working for ourselves.

Needs

The fortunate ones are those who enjoy doing the jobs for which they are paid. The less fortunate, and there are many of these, simply sell their services as a means to an end — earning money in order to live. In such cases, where there may be little satisfaction in actually doing the job, other factors may help to compensate:

1. In working life — good working conditions, pleasant colleagues, long holidays or 'perks'.
2. In social life — absorbing interests, good personal relationships, even community involvement.

If job dissatisfaction becomes extreme, it may lead people into seeking opportunities for re-training at any age and, in fact, some mature students enter the secretarial field for this reason.

When it becomes impossible to sell one's services, even though basic needs may be met by the provision of unemployment benefit (food, shelter, clothing), other needs are frustrated — the sense of belonging, of purpose, of respect *from*

Where do I go from here?

other people and, perhaps the most important of all, one's self-respect and self-esteem. For most of us then, selling our sevices is important.

Are secretarial skills marketable?

In choosing to do a secretarial course, perhaps straight from school after 'CSE', 'O', or 'A' levels, after a degree course, or as a mature student changing direction, you have no doubt realized that although in some regions the choice of jobs may not be as wide as in former years, the prospects for employment remain good. In opting for secretarial work, there is a degree of security not present in many jobs especially if you are willing and able to travel to different parts of the country or to work overseas.

While there is no clearly defined career structure in secretarial work and, in the majority of cases, your job will be supportive, there are a number of directions in which you may decide to go:

1. Within the job itself opportunities may present themselves to broaden the scope of your capabilities by taking on extra responsibility and using your initiative.

2. By making yourself indispensable to your boss, you could remain with him as he is promoted or move with him to a more senior appointment with another company.

3. As you gain experience, you may feel you want to take on the challenge of a more demanding job either with a different type of organization or with a higher level of management.

4. As you become more knowledgeable about the company and its future plans, you may decide to specialize and find your way into junior management. (Some examinations such as the RSA Diploma for Personal Assistants could provide a foundation for entry into the specialist fields.)

5. The opportunity may even arise for you to take on your boss's job!

Local opportunities

If domestic commitments or personal preferences limit you to a particular geographical area then clearly your opportunities will be restricted to those available in *that* area.

By studying advertisements in local newspapers, by applying to local job centres or private agencies, or hearing by word of mouth, you should become aware of any vacancies that exist.

It is possible that your first job may not come up to your expectations but you will be gaining that much needed 'experience' and you *will* be earning while learning.

If a particular local firm appeals to you for one reason or another, direct application could result in an invitation to attend for interview even if no vacancy exists at that time. You have shown initiative by writing and if, added to this, you make a good impression and a good job of selling yourself at the interview, you will be remembered when a vacancy does arise!

When you are called for interview, you should study any information you can about the firm in your local library before you attend. Some libraries keep press cuttings and other information for just this purpose. Research for information on the products made or the services offered, number of employees, profit figures and, if possible, future plans.

If no opportunity presents itself by the time you leave college then you could consider temporary work, which is nearly always available during the summer months when permanent staff go on holiday. Remember though that you must be very adaptable and flexible — able to adjust to meeting new people, coping with new machinery, finding your way around new surroundings, and learning different terminology and house styles, possibly every other week.

Temporary work may be a challenge; you will gain valuable experience and insight into a number of different types of business. You may even be offered a permanent job!

Have skills — will travel

As you will have realized by now, there is no end to the variety of businesses and organizations that employ secretaries. If you are able to travel and especially if you can offer one or two languages then you will obviously enhance your job prospects. You may be able to turn your particular hobbies or interests to advantage and, allied with your skills, find a job in which you will start with a real involvement.

Secretarial linguists will find opportunities in London and overseas and very good agencies exist to provide contacts. Also the status of secretaries in many countries of the world is greater than it is in England. A UK-trained English-speaking secretary is considered to be a great asset and is rewarded accordingly.

Companionship your need?

The Women's Services — WRAC, WRAF, and WRNS — usually have vacancies for shorthand writers with speeds of around 100 w.p.m. shorthand and 50 w.p.m. typing and the qualities of commonsense, initiative, integrity, and maturity. You may have or may acquire the necessary qualifications to commissioned service.

The Diplomatic Service undertakes direct recruitment, and selection to the secretarial branch is by personal interview at which the applicants must pass tests at 100 w.p.m. shorthand and 30 w.p.m. typing. A new entrant first works in one of the departments of the Foreign and Commonwealth Office in London before being posted overseas at the age of 20 or 21.

Your aim to specialize?

Although you may be completing or have completed a non-specialist secretarial course, you may have developed an interest in being a medical secretary. Further information on training and prospects may be obtained from the Association of Medical Secretaries, Tavistock House South, Tavistock Square, London WC1H 9LN.

If you live in the country, you may feel that you want to specialize in being a farm secretary and if so The Institute of Agricultural Secretaries, 16a Market

Place, Chipping Norton, Oxfordshire will be able to help you.

Open to suggestions?

Many secretaries are interested in the media and the fields of advertising and journalism. Some quality newspapers have specialist days when advertisements concentrate on particular types of job although they tend to be in the south-east region. This might be another occasion when direct application could pay off.

Trade magazines and other specialist magazines carry advertisements for secretarial vacancies — some offering accommodation — and you can probably find these in your local library. By studying them you will become aware of the types of job available and how they may be combined with your particular needs and interests.

You may have an interest in working in a school, a college, a hotel, in social work, in charity work, in advertising, in publishing, in insurance — the list is endless. Remember the least glamorous sounding job could be the most interesting.

You and only you know your expectations, your hopes, your needs. You must be realistic and honest in your self-appraisal, aware of your limitations and weaknesses. Perhaps more importantly, you should know your strong points and how you can exploit these to achieve a greater sense of fulfilment.

Whether you become a large cog in a small wheel or a small cog in a large wheel, you are an individual and as such you will make a valuable contribution to the company for which you will work.

If you doubt your importance as an individual, consider how useless your typewriter would be with only one faulty key.

Xvxn if only onx kxy doxs not work corrxctly it would bx hopxlxss to xndxavour to producx typxwrittxn mattxr which would bx of usx.

Your solx xffort is as nxcxssary as that onx kxy to thx ovxrall xfficixncy and xffxctivxnxss of your txam.

YOU ARX RXALLY XSSXNTIAL

(With acknowledgments to an unknown author for borrowing the idea.)

Do you know?

1. Your geographical limitations — local (10 mile radius), within travelling distance (30 miles), or unlimited (willing to move and to travel)?
2. Whether you want to stay in this country or to travel overseas?
3. The particular field in which you would like to work, e.g., legal, medical, media, engineering, public relations, leisure, or any others?
4. What are your particular strengths?

Snippets

1. The Institute of Qualified Private Secretaries (IQPS) aims to establish the status of the qualified private secretary and is represented in all parts of the country by regional branches. The IQPS has been granted membership of the British Institute of Management.
2. Recruitment to the Commission of European Communities (typists and secretaries) is made by advertisements in a number of papers among which are *The Times, Daily Telegraph, Glasgow Herald* and the *Irish Independent.*
3. The Executive Secretaries Association aims, among other things, to promote the status of executive secretaries, to provide a forum for discussion and exchange of ideas, advice, and support, to investigate new technology, and to liaise with other secretarial associations at home and abroad.
4. The Association of Personal Assistants and Secretaries Limited was formed to improve the status and to offer advice on professional matters to those engaged in PA or secretarial work.
5. The Eurotech Management Development Service regularly runs seminars for working secretaries. 'The Secretary's Role as a Personal Assistant' for instance, is intended for the secretary who has had two or more years' experiencee working for senior management.
6. The European Association of Professional Secretaries aims among other things 'to be the recognized voice of the secretarial profession in Europe'.
7. Many colleges provide part-time courses for working secretaries to improve their qualifications and hence their career prospects.

During the next few weeks, make a study of secretarial opportunities along the following lines:

1. Jobs in your area in large companies and small using all of the suggested sources.
2. National opportunities in general and in the particular business in which you are interested at home and overseas.
3. Extract any articles giving information on developments in the type of organization in which you are interested.
4. Research additional careers that are open to you after successfully completing a secretarial course, e.g., teaching.
5. Do an analysis of the wording of advertisements in all sources and discover how many euphemisms there are for 'secretaries'.
6. Consider any additional skills that would be beneficial for you to have, e.g., driving.

Index

Communications:
  audio, 155, 158, 162
  comparison, 20
  fax, 16, 157, 160, 165
  grapevine, 119, 143
  mailing shots, 16
  media, 14
  networks, 160
  pagers, 155, 164
  telephones, 16, 145, 155, 157, 158, 163, 166
  telex, 15, 16, 159, 163
Conferences:
  calls, 157
  industry, 41
  organization, 39, 40, 42, 45-49
  press, 41
  purpose, 40, 41, 42
Confidentiality, 130, 131
  precautions, 130-132

Disabled, 30, 32, 163

Electronic office, 155-166
  attitudes, 162
  terminology, 164-165
Environment:
  colour, 27, 28, 30
  ergonomics, 30
  furniture, 27, 28, 86, 155
  legal requirements, 28, 30, 139, 140
  noise, 27, 28, 29
Exhibitions (see Trade Fairs)

Filing:
  electronic, 160
  handover, 88-89
  hardware, 84
  methods, 94, 95
  microforms, 85, 86, 163
  procedure, 84, 85, 86
  reorganization, 89-93
  systems, 83, 85
  training, 86-88

Human relations, 142-143
  personality clashes, 4
  role adjustment, 4
  self-criticism, 4, 143
  personality types, 4, 147-148

Information centres, 156

Job:
  interviews, 173-174
  needs, 171
  opportunities, 173-174
  qualifications, 172-173
  satisfaction, 141-142, 144-145

Mail, electronic, 158-159, 166
Meetings:
  annual general, 53, 55
  chairman, 52
  committee secretary, 52
  informal, 54
  minutes, 55
  oranization, 57-66
  preparation, 52-55
  procedure, 56, 57
  secretary, 52
  validity, 55
Microprocessors, 155, 156, 157

Performance, factors affecting, 29, 31, 33, 141, 142-143
Personnel:
  induction, 167-168
  interviews, 140, 142
  origins, 139-140
  self-appraisal, 142
  supervision, 141-142, 143-145
Problems, additional, 9, 12, 13, 19, 24, 35, 37, 38, 49, 50, 51, 63, 67, 76, 80, 93, 96, 106, 115, 117, 126, 129, 134, 136, 149, 152, 170
Problems, long:
  communication media, 18
  computer bureau, 126

Problems, long:—*continued*
  conference organization, 45
  devising filing system, 93
  flexitime, 149
  house magazine, 19
  human relations, 7, 10
  importing agencies, 105
  induction, 167
  journey, Europe, 71
  journey, trade fair, 76
  loyalty, 134
  meetings organization, 57, 63
  office organization, 32
  reorganization, filing, 89
  safety and health, 115
  safety rules, 114
  security leak, 123
  supervisory, 146
  word processors, 36
Problems, short:
  accident, 6
  delegation, 143
  disabled, 31
  equipment, electronic office, 164
  interview, 6
  loyalty, 132
  meetings procedure, 55
  meetings terminology, 55
  obtaining current information, 102, 104
  operating new filing system, 86
  performance appraisal, 143
  quotations, 102
  safety notices, 111
  security, 122, 132
  telephone, 16
  terminology, electronic office, 164
  tidiness, 31
  trade fair, 43
  training junior, filing, 86
  travel safeguards, 69
  urgent reorganization, 43

Professional bodies, 102, 103, 121-122, 128, 176

Reference:
  books, 69, 97, 98, 101, 102
  bureaux, 101, 126-129
  business sources, 98, 99, 101, 103
  business TV, 99, 100
  libraries, 97, 99, 100, 102
  press, 97, 98, 99, 101, 103
  sources, 98, 99, 100, 102
Reprographics, 157, 163, 166, 167

Safety:
  hazards, 110, 111, 115
  legislation, 109, 110, 111, 112
  precautions, 112, 113, 116-117
  responsibility, 110
Secretary, 3, 40, 97, 120
  junior executive, 3
  personal assistant, 3
Security:
  devices, 121, 158
  of information, 119
  precautions, 119, 121-122
  responsibility, 119

Trade fairs, 42, 43-45, 76
Travel:
  arrangements, 68, 69, 69-75, 78-79
  documents, 68, 69, 70, 75, 78
  international dateline, 69
  itinerary, 74
  reference books, 69
  trade missions, 69
Typewriters, electronic, 161, 163, 167

Word processors, 28, 31, 36-37, 86, 120, 132, 156,
  159, 161, 163, 167